IF ONLY YOU PEOPLE COULD FOLLOW DIRECTIONS

IF ONLY YOU PEOPLE COULD FOLLOW DIRECTIONS

A MEMOIR

JESSICA HENDRY NELSON

COUNTERPOINT · BERKELEY, CALIFORNIA

Library of Congress Cataloging-in-Publication Data

Nelson, Jessica Hendry.
If only you people could follow directions : a memoir / Jessica Hendry
Nelson.
pages cm
1. Nelson, Jessica Hendry. 2. Nelson, Jessica Hendry—Family.
3. Children of drug addicts—Biography. 4. Children of parents with
mental disabilities—Biography. I. Title.
CT275.N44276A3 2013
362.3'3092—dc23
[B]
2013028331

ISBN 978-1-61902-233-1

Cover design by Michael Fusco
Interior design by Neuwirth & Associates

COUNTERPOINT
1919 Fifth Street
Berkeley, CA 94710
www.counterpointpress.com

Printed in the United States of America
Distributed by Publishers Group West

10 9 8 7 6 5 4 3 2 1

For my mother, Susan, my brother, Eric, and Nick.

TABLE OF CONTENTS

IF ONLY YOU PEOPLE COULD FOLLOW DIRECTIONS

PROLOGUE

A LETTER TO ERIC

YOU AND I visit our father on Saturdays between the hours of one and two. We visit him alongside the other children and the other fathers. The building is low and concrete, and we visit outside. We visit him wearing blue jeans and wool sweaters and new sneakers. It is 1989. It is 1991. It is 1992 and then it is 1995. It is Livengrin Foundation for Addiction Recovery or it is The Caron Foundation or it is this rehab or that. It is by farmland and fences and old graveyards and small airports. Mothers like ours wait in the car, or else they sit beside the children and kiss their men on the mouth and stroke the children's hair. Everyone sits at picnic tables on the lawn and the fathers talk and smoke and the children listen and are shy. Most of the men wear mustaches and tan work boots and flannel shirts. They look like they've only just put down their hammers for a quick lunch and a chat, while behind them some new house might be teetering dangerously, all stud-stripped and soft concrete. The men look interrupted, rather than finished, and maybe that's what we find so surprising. Our father looks baffled, as I imagine that Mexican farmer looked when the Paricutin volcano appeared in his cornfield overnight. That was 1943. I'm reading about it in school. These things happen, they tell us. One day you wake up and find a giant stinking hole where your life used to be.

WE VISIT HIM in the hospital at three in the morning and eat bags of chips from the vending machine. It is 1990. We wear our pajamas under our coats and play tic-tac-toe on the backs of our mother's crumpled receipts. We are giddy to be up so late. We feel like explorers in a parallel universe, a place children seldom go, and we plan to report back. When he comes into the waiting room, he looks just like our father, only minus two teeth and with a nose we hadn't imagined could get any crookeder. We give him hugs and potato chips. He smiles with his lips closed, then he starts to speak and we get scared and cry. His mouth is a deep red cave with shards of teeth dangling like stalactites, which I am also reading about in school.

WE VISIT HIM in their room one morning and crawl under the blankets and he says, "What is this? What are these lumps in my bed?" and pats our wriggling heads and backs and bottoms, and we bounce around and laugh so hard we knock our heads together. It is 1989.

WE VISIT HIM in jail and bring a deck of cards, your soccer trophy, and a carton of Camel Lights. The guards make us leave it all in a box at the desk and we forget to take your trophy on the way out. It is 1992. It is the Montgomery County Correctional Facility or it is the Bucks County Correctional Facility. It is drunk driving or petty theft or unpaid child support. You cry for hours over your trophy, hiccupping and drooling, until we turn on *The Flintstones* and you forget. When the show is over you look at me in surprise and start in again, but your heart's not in it.

WE VISIT HIM in another rehab and watch football on a small TV with no sound. He introduces us to his friends and he looks proud, and they smile politely and clap our shoulders. He offers us gifts—a keychain with a dangling pink peace sign, packs of Starburst candy, an old *Highlights* magazine with some doctor's address on the white sticker, a rubber refrigerator magnet of Joe Camel in sunglasses shooting pool with the word "Smooth" emblazoned on his T-shirt—everything wrapped neatly in newspaper. He offers us coffee from a big silver pot and you say, okay, sure, even though you're only eight, and he pours some into a Styrofoam cup and hands it to you and you dump it out later when he goes to the bathroom. It is 1994.

WE VISIT HIM at Grandma's big house and we take her car and go out for spaghetti and meatballs and ice cream. It is 1996. He asks us about school and later we wonder why grown-ups only want to talk about school. When we get back he pulls too far into the garage and we hit the wall with a gentle crunch and he backs up a little and parks and nobody says boo and we go inside.

WE VISIT HIM at the halfway house and sit on his very own bed and meet more men with mustaches. You show him some of your magic tricks and he is amazed every time you pick his card and every time you don't. It is 1997.

WE VISIT HIM at his brother's house after the baby dies and you are a perfect gentleman, a little man, like grief is a language you have perfected at twelve, and Aunt Kim holds on to you like the dickens while Dad and Uncle David snort pills upstairs and quietly go mad. It is 1999.

WE VISIT HIM in the city as teenagers and he greets us at the train station and we walk around for hours. It is 2000. He gives us cigarettes. We buy hoagies with the money Mom gave us and sit on a bench next to the Delaware River and watch the rowers pull black oars through black water. He tells us he spends most of his time at the public library and that he might have a job building big houses for rich people. I hold my breath every time we pass a bar because I do not yet understand that addiction has nothing to do with neon signs, which I imagine blinking on and off inside his chest like an electric heart.

WE VISIT HIM at his friend's apartment where he is sleeping on the couch and we eat bags of wet popcorn and watch movies until late at night. We listen to him on the phone in the kitchen telling someone about our neighbor, my friend's mom, who tried to seduce him in a hotel room with bottles of vodka and Klonopin, and he doesn't even whisper and we always remember that he didn't even whisper. It is 2001. When she kills herself a few years later, nobody's whispering anymore.

LESS OFTEN, HE visits us.

HE VISITS US at home sometimes, when Mom is there to supervise. It is 1998. I spend a long time preparing my outfit: a long skirt and a hot-pink blouse. I wait for him on the corner of our street and when he drives by in the passenger seat of a friend's rusted-out truck he doesn't recognize me—that's how long it's been—and whistles out the window, *woohoo*, wind whipping back his blond hair, his big fingers in his mouth, and I can't help it; I feel grown up and too proud.

HE VISITS US on the day I am not accepted to travel to Japan with the smart kids at school and I am crying so loudly and he hugs me to his chest. It is 1997. "My poor Lumps," he says, because that's what he calls me after the whole crawling-under-the-blanket thing, which happened not just once but all the time. You are "Pumpkin" because your head was shaped like a pumpkin, and I used to want to crack your pumpkin head open with my fist, Pumpkin, and mostly I still do.

HE VISITS US at soccer and baseball and softball practices when Mom isn't there and she yells at him later. One time, he signs up to be my softball coach. It is 1996. I am blue daisies, but then he doesn't make it to the first game and the assistant coach takes over and nobody talks about what happened to our dad and I am embarrassed, like the time he stole all the cookie money from my Girl Scout troop and let Mom take all the blame.

HE VISITS US in our dreams and sometimes he has a mustache and sometimes he doesn't. We talk about it together and say, *Remember this?* and *Remember that?* It is 2002 and it will never end. We say, *Remember the time he shaved his mustache and came down to breakfast and nobody noticed for a while and then you noticed and cried out, "Dad doesn't have a top lip!"* which was true enough, and then he grew it back and never shaved it off again.

HE VISITS US when we are so stoned and driving through the neighborhood in reverse and listening to his favorite songs and talking about the time when I was nine and you were seven and we went door-to-door selling off his tape collection for a dollar apiece. It is 2000. That was 1990. But of course we got caught and had to go back to each house and return the sweaty, balled-up dollar bills from our pockets, which we held out in our trembling palms like peace offerings.

WE ARE SUPPOSED to visit him one day, again at Grandma's, and we head over there in my first car—the little Nissan, remember? But then we decide to run home first and grab something, who knows what, and Mom's there and she's a mess and we find out he died and you lock yourself in your room for three days. When you come out you are high as the sky and you haven't come down yet. It is April 4, 2002.

NOW, HE VISITS us first thing in the morning when we are drinking our coffee in our separate apartments in our separate cities in our separate states.

HE VISITS US when we are happy and when we are sad.

HE VISITS US every time you land in the same jail, your twin mug shots forever floating in the same county database, each one more fucked up than the last.

HE VISITS US when we are broke down and blacked out and beaten up. When we are bringing more dead bodies to the same cemetery. When we are eating pizza with pepperoni. When we are playing cards or fishing or on a boat, anywhere at any time. When Grandma died this past winter and you were newly sober and held my hand the whole time like the big man you were becoming. When we are on the street and it is crowded and there are blond men with mustaches ducking into corner stores to buy cigarettes. When we are chewing spearmint gum or at a shoe store or a Jiffy Lube. When we see men in orange vests picking up trash on the side of a highway. When we are walking through woods or down alleyways. When I hear your voice for the first time in a long time and startle at how much you sound like him. Whenever the Indigo Girls come on the radio. Or Led Zeppelin. Or Genesis. When we pet a black lab and when we eat chicken pot pie. When we see a pickup truck. When I read Steinbeck. When you watch *Mash*.

SO, HERE'S TO the big-bellied men in flannel, to huge clumsy hands of stillborn blue. To the choked-up, spit-out slide of attrition. To the housebuilders and the homewreckers. To the jokesters and the dream crashers and the old-timey tinkers. To the wrench pullers and car wreckers. To the name givers and the frozen-pie makers. Here's to the fold, to the snug saltbox houses on dead-end streets that he loved so well. Here's to oil-packed cans of tuna fish that will pass for a meal and the ghostly women who give them away.

HERE'S TO THIS night in Vermont and the snow burying the birdseed and the silver pickerel frozen in the lake, tiny half-moons of perfect comedy and perfect tragedy.

HERE'S TO OUR dead, flickering in and out of focus, like ashes from long extinguished volcanoes that somehow make it across time and oceans to land in our cereal. Something like that.

AND HERE'S TO you, Pumpkin, wherever you are.

—February 23, 2012

HERE,
FISHY
FISHY

A FEW DAYS after our father is arrested near our home outside of Philadelphia, I find a Bible in the nightstand drawer. This is our third night in this New Jersey Shore motel room and we are getting restless. We are tired and stoned and our mother sleeps on the other twin bed with her mouth open, snoring loudly. I am fifteen, Eric is thirteen, and we are at home wherever we land, the three of us, together. Here, the window shades are heavy and purple and dust crowds a slip of light. I am sleepless and giddy. Eric opens the Bible. Many of the paragraphs are underlined and with such force that the pages are ripped and stained ink blue. This is a dark and quiet hour and there is flickering from a muted television. Eric whispers passages to me and we laugh like much younger children. We don't read Bibles, don't need Bibles, don't feel anything but the pulse of the weed and a wet wind that blows past the blinds. I touch my brother's cheek to see if his skin is as hot as it looks, pinprick red, as if all of his blood is being lured to the surface by the damp heat in this room. My brother's complexion is darker than mine anyway, kissed by the whisper of Eastern European roots, while I am like my father, fair-haired and pig-belly pink.

This room, it hums with the promise of rain.

"Here," I say, "feel my head," and he does, squinting at me and deciding we feel just the same.

I know suddenly we will paint our toenails black and my brother says, "All right then, do mine."

When we were little kids, our father often hooked a tiny sailboat to the back of his truck and drove two hours to Chesapeake Bay. It was a Sunfish with a bright-yellow hull. He taught us to sail around the peninsula while my mother fished from shore. She waved at us every time we turned around, her cigarette bouncing between her fingers like a rock 'n' roll song. The Sunfish didn't last long, rusting away in the backyard like some overgrown lawn ornament, so my father's old-money parents started chartering boats for the whole family. We sailed all over the Chesapeake Bay for weeks at a time, eating the thick stew that my grandmother would thaw on an electric burner each night. I remember I wore the same white dress every day because I liked the way it blew in the wind when I stood on the bow of the boat. When the warm air whipped through my hair and up my thighs, I felt my first shudders of romance. Often, I would kneel down and wrap my arms tightly around my knees until I felt something like leeches, swollen and slick with blood, slide down my thighs, my crooked little toes. The harder I squeezed, the more powerful I felt. I thought myself a *renegade*, which is a word I'd read in *Anne of Green Gables* and took to mean something akin to royalty, though I wasn't sure how. Also, I liked the feel of the letters in my mouth, the rolling consonants and the hard suffix. *Ade, blade, swayed.* I could rhyme for hours, watching the tops of my feet change colors in the sun.

What a stark contrast to our lives back home, in the suburbs of Philadelphia, where everything looked like the dirty underside of a couch cushion and evenings were spent in the back room of Skip's, the bar around the corner. Not that we minded Skip's much. At least we were allowed bowls of peanuts and oversweet Shirley Temples. Occasionally, Dad would hand Eric and me a fistful of quarters for the pool table, which we didn't know how to play, but we enjoyed making up our own games anyway. We'd sit cross-legged on top of the green felt and let our knees clack together, a sound like hollowed-out chicken bones. First person to fit a whole pool ball into his or her mouth won. Or we'd pretend the blue chalk was war paint and I'd draw arrows across my brother's smooth forehead, cartoon skulls on his cheeks. Later, we'd squeeze into the cab of Dad's pickup truck and wend our way home, six blocks at five miles per hour, reeking of cigarette smoke and spearmint gum and belting "American Pie." Our mother's parents paid the rent for the small, two-bedroom ranch house we lived in, all brick and linoleum and brown shag carpets. It was half an hour from Philadelphia and five minutes from them. We lived at the bottom of the street, the least affluent part of the neighborhood, which grew increasingly middle class as you ascended the hill. Our neighbors were mechanics, grocery store clerks, barbers, construction workers, bartenders. They were mostly white. There was a lot of stuff everywhere; I remember that. Old cars on jacks, broken toys and lawn ornaments, tires and tools and creaky swing sets. I could see the city skyline when it was clear. I would run around barefoot all day.

We ate lots of stew on those sailboats on the bay, and we listened to the tapes that my father liked best. Bonnie Raitt, Led Zeppelin, the Indigo Girls. We crabbed in the marshes, and I remember my mother being dismayed by how much Eric and I enjoyed dropping crabs into boiling water, my brother poking at them with a wooden spoon as they tried to escape, while I screamed and giggled and kicked at the stove like a maniac. In the mornings, my father let us steer the boat while he trimmed the sails, ducking beneath the boom and quickly wrapping the rope around his arm. He moved fluidly, assuredly, manipulating the huge Island Packet as if tuning a violin.

When my father was still young and whip-smart and licking his wounds with alcohol, his parents paid a large sum of money so that he could join a crew from New England that sailed down to the islands of the Bahamas. He'd been a solemn boy, too much in his head, and he'd felt a nameless pain he was too proud to mention. It was grotesque, like something left out to rot, and so he kept this hazy sorrow to himself and used booze to dress it up for a day, a night, a few goddamn hours. This was before the days of AA, of higher powers and twelve steps and endless Styrofoam cups of coffee grinds and cigarette butts. Before babies and their shit-heavy diapers, wet mouths, and oversized heads. Before talk therapy. Before asbestos removal jobs and wrecked cars. Nights so hot and black they burned like a solar eclipse through his insides. Before little league games and parent-teacher conferences. Before he fucked the three-hundred-pound housewife next door for a couple of Klonopin. Before she killed herself with the rest.

Before all that, I imagine him long-limbed and cherry red in the sun, tossing ropes to shore and tying his Boy Scout knots—a doomed, affable expression beneath curls of Nordic white hair. With his right hand he tosses the anchor into the water, feeling for the weight and dredge of the sand, the faintest vibration, the last job well done. He leans back against the mast and lights a cigarette and surveys this new velvet landscape, colors he hadn't imagined could be so saturated, and then tosses the pack to a friend.

It's March and we should be in school but we're not. This isn't unusual. Even though our father hasn't lived with us for years, my mother still thinks it best to take off every time he "falls off the wagon" and gets arrested, as if distance alone could protect us. This time it's drinking and driving and unpaid fines from previous arrests for drinking and driving. There were a couple of sober years, when Eric and I were in early elementary school. Since then, he's had at least two DUIs a year, and he cycles from jail to rehab to halfway house and back again. Occasionally, he'll manage a few sober months in a halfway house, and occasionally he'll stay with his mother in anticipation of getting his own place. During those months, there is lots of talk about the future, of our own bedrooms and weekends spent watching movies and skiing at the Pocono Mountains, but it never happens.

"Same old, same old," Eric sings, *woo woo woo.*

The drive from Philadelphia to the Jersey Shore takes nearly two hours. We know it well; we do this at least twice a year.

Eric always falls asleep the moment we leave the driveway and wakes up, as if by instinct, the second we cross the bridge into Sea Isle City. Today when we arrive there aren't many fishermen—it's still too early in the season—but a few grizzled diehards lean heavily on the bridge's steel railings, hooking their lines with wet strips of haddock or hunks of clam. Or else they sit on overturned buckets with one hand on the rod, the other holding a sandwich made with white bread, and watch the tide turn. Eric and I always make a game out of who can spot the first catch, the angry curve of the flounder's belly like a silver scythe in the sun. There is something heroic about fishermen—all that faith in the dark.

The bridge trembles as we speed across it, the men frozen in their various postures; our car shoots into the sky.

We rent putt-putts, as Dad used to call them, every summer when we're down the Jersey Shore. That's what we say in Philly: not "at the Shore," but "down the Shore." They are tiny, sputtering things with single engines that just manage to get us from the dock on the bay over to the nearby marshes where fish are hiding in the grass roots. A home video features one of these early trips. My mother is doing her first "Voodoo Fisherwoman" routine for the camera—a subtle performance—her eyes squeezed shut, her lips pursed like a fish. Slowly and meditatively, she calls the fish to her line.

"Here, fishy fishy fishy," she whispers. "Here, fishy fishy."

My father laughs convulsively in the background, one hand on the engine, the other holding a can of Budweiser. Eric looks up at him and laughs, clearly more excited by his father's ebullience than his mother's performance. I smile girlishly from behind the camera before inexplicably holding up a peace sign in front of the lens, as if anticipating the brevity of these good times. *All here together!* I might be trying to say.

IN THE MOTEL room, we don't talk about where our father went or why. Because I don't know better, I envision the process of entering jail to be like checking into a hotel. I see my father walking up to the desk of his own accord and receiving a key to his room, following an old woman with puffy red hair down a dark hallway, and trailing his old corduroy suitcase behind him. Or maybe it is more like the rehabs we used to visit— large, empty lobbies and television sets that were always on mute. Outside, clusters of unshaven men in blue jeans and flannel shirts sit around picnic tables smoking and playing cards. It was at one of these rehabs that I learned how to play poker, the only card game I still play well.

The next morning we eat sticky buns on the beach and rinse caramel and shredded napkin from our fingers in the frigid water. All along the Jersey Shore it is overcast and chilly, but not yet raining. We watch the sandpipers chase a receding wave, ecstatically pecking at the sand until the tide turns, a deep breath, the next wave exhaling and tumbling after the birds. They skitter away in unison, legs straight as stilts. The planet's longest-running game of tag.

"We okay? Everyone okay?" She is checking, again.

We are still okay. Eric wants to go watch girls dance in bikinis. We heard on television that somewhere nearby MTV is taping its Spring Break Special. This is part of the reason we have come to Sea Isle rather than Ocean City, where we usually go. The other part has to do with unfamiliar terrain and liberation, our mother thinking the two identical. Eric is too young to get into the MTV dance party, he tells me later, but he will watch the girls through slats in a fence until a big man with an earpiece chases him away. Mom wants to read her book on a bench near the boardwalk, under the red and white Johnson's Popcorn awning. I tell her I'm going to the beach to do some homework. I am fifteen now, I argue, and can spend some time *alone for christsake.* She looks at me, tired, and nods. We are all tired. I take off down an alleyway to smoke cigarettes and search for reusable trash. I find an empty inkwell near a chain-link fence and consider it a good day. The bottle's opening looks like two hungry, porcelain lips and suggests an era I've never known but suddenly miss, like a phantom limb or an estranged twin.

Sea Isle looks like an abandoned circus; electric signs pulse into the fog like lighthouses. Old men huddle outside brick bars in twos and threes while cigarette smoke drifts out of open doorways into the morning. A spitting rain coats the sidewalk. I notice a storefront that reads We Sell Beer and Gold. Several blocks west, a cop slowly crosses the intersection on a black horse, the beast's tail whipping at low clouds as they turn down another alleyway and amble out of view. I'm sure I am losing my mind.

According to the local news, this is the first of many days of rain. Gutters churn. A pair of seagulls pick at the trash that is tossed out of curbside streams. We could drown in fog so thick. When I find Eric he is huddled behind an empty shake shack trying to light a joint with a pack of matches. He is hunched over and haggard-looking, like a bit of flotsam cast out from an errant tide. I don't ask about his missing shoe.

"Where's Mom?" he says, picking a loose pot leaf from his tongue.

He is crouched very low to the ground and in this position he resembles an old man. He is a pale kid, skinny and tall. Lately, the flush of adolescence has drained from his cheeks. Instead, gray pools of exhaustion settle beneath his eyes. His hair is always messy now, even when he tries to gel the bangs straight up into the air—as if he's in the habit of running into walls.

"I don't know. Probably trying to flirt her way on to MTV."

We are angry at her these days, though neither of us could say exactly why. Probably it is easier to beat up the parent who is close enough to field the blows. Last week she came home drunk at five o'clock in the afternoon and ordered us both to bed. It was the first time we'd ever seen her drunk, and we are hell-bent on never letting her forget it. There is only room for one addict in this family, and that position was filled years ago.

"I lost my shoe," Eric says.

"I see that."

"Hit?" He holds out the joint, a sloppy job that smokes too much on one side.

Eventually, a day will come when I realize with horror that I was the one to introduce my little brother to drugs—handing him his first joint at twelve, sneaking out with him in the midnight hours to take hits from a pipe made from an apple, heaving barrels of change to the local Coinstar to finance the evening's entertainment. But now, that day is still very far away. Now, we are still a team. He hasn't yet lost control and we can still distract ourselves with games of hide-and-seek, run-and-return, here-I-am-now-I'm-not.

"Nah," I say. "But can I have your other shoe since you don't really need it now?"

I've been thinking about his shoes a lot lately, real dark leather and long as platters, the shoelaces missing. I've considered adding them to my collection of planters made from old shoes, which are clustered on my windowsill. I felt the shoe pots added a real sense of irony to the space, and Mom agreed, until I planted yellow geraniums in her only red pumps. I'd been reading *A Tree Grows in Brooklyn* and the shoe pots became my homage to the central metaphor, and also to Francie, who I imagined as my spirit sister. *Our daddies even have the same name!* I thought. *Our daddies don't have jobs!*

"A Geranium Grows in Funk," I wrote on an index card and taped it to the wall next to the window.

I once glued pieces of a broken mirror to the wall above my

bed, the shards of glass positioned to look like an exploding heart. For weeks, I shuddered through dreams, tiny cuts forming down my abdomen, and woke up with pieces of glass in my hair. Eventually, I gave up and took it down. I inserted the shards into some of the dark earth in my shoe pots. In the winter light they look like melting glaciers.

MY BROTHER AND I walk down Ocean Avenue toward the boardwalk, Eric shoeless, both of us tiptoeing around broken bottles, paper bags, and chicken bones. I make him hold my hand, not because I am particularly fond of him, but because it looks to all the world like I have a boyfriend. And there is nothing I want more than to look like I have a boyfriend. A girl with backup. I have no idea how to relate to boys other than my brother, so a real boyfriend is out of the question. It would just be nice to *look* involved, like Carrie Kid and Chris Caruthers, who stumble down school hallways as if they're in a three-legged race. I am in love with both of them on different days.

We pass a man sitting inside a wooden hutch at the entrance to an empty parking lot. He doesn't lift his head as we shuffle by. He is reading a paperback that is swollen with moisture, the pages buckled like waves. He doesn't seem to notice the shutters banging in the wind, the warm rain sliding down the back of his neck.

Eric takes off his T-shirt and ties it in a knot around his waist. I press on the round fist of bone at the top of his spine. *What a curious boy*, I think. He has a hang-dog neck like a marionette. He bats my hand away as we enter the arcade on the boardwalk. The kid behind the counter watches us as we walk down the aisles, poking buttons and fingering plastic guns. We look like vagabonds, road-weary immigrants suddenly deported to this dank and derelict tourist town, this aqueous vortex with caramel corn.

Just let me rest my head inside this race car, I think. *I'd like to take this spaceship for a ride.*

On the fifth morning Mom is up especially early.

"Rise and shine!" she says, ripping at our blankets.

I heard her get up to use the bathroom so I am prepared, wrapping the cheap polyester blanket around me like a tortilla. Eric isn't so lucky and he thrashes at the air and moans while our mother bunches up his covers and draws back the heavy curtains, asking which one of us would like to go get her coffee. We know this isn't really a question, so we stage a silent protest.

"All right," she chirps, "then I guess I'm going fishing alone," which is enough, she knows, to at least get us to open our eyes.

We don't ask when we're going home because, we figure, anything is better than being in school. Plus, we love fishing.

She leaves us to shower and get dressed while she drives to a neighboring shore town to see about a boat. Right after she leaves I notice the money missing from my wallet, and I turn on Eric with alarming ferocity. Stealing is a new habit of his, but my occasional violence toward him is not novel. I have a very early memory of choking my brother until he turned blue. He couldn't have been more than two years old. Choking was one of my favorite methods of assault, my scrawny brother writhing as I held him on the ground, my knees pressed deep into his stomach. I wasn't satisfied until he cried, and I never worried about rebuttal. His counterattacks were fruitless, and if he ever got particularly aggressive, I would simply roll onto my back and fend him off with a barrage of kicks, like a lizard spreading her wattle to ward off predators.

"Really, Jess? Ten bucks? You're going apeshit over ten bucks?" His voice gets louder; he squints as if he can't quite make me out.

My mother warned me this day would come; I just didn't expect it so soon. "One day," she'd said, "he's gonna be bigger than you. You'll try to beat him up and he'll kick your ass from here to next Tuesday."

I realize I'm in trouble when he doesn't start to cry. Eric has always been a big crier. He is sensitive to his surroundings; a slight change in air pressure can set him off. He sidles into the bathroom and I follow him. I really want that $10 back. I really want an apology and everlasting repentance, some acknowledgment of my moral superiority at least. I want this scraggly, petty thief to bow down in his too-small undershirt and pledge undying supplication. In the absence of all of these concessions, I see no other choice but to attack.

I catch myself in the mirror, a feral child, hair wild and teeth bared, a line of spittle down my chin. There is a scuffle. I hear the crack of his spine as he lands backward in the tub. His skull bounces off the green linoleum wall. He does not immediately react, but he appears completely composed, breathing deeply and staring right through me. I'm screwed and I know it.

A few weeks before our father was arrested and the three of us took off into exile, my brother and I went to see an art exhibit in the city. It is the sort of experience that wasn't immediately appealing, but in contrast to school, well, it gave us something to do. We jumped on the train during school hours and planned to be back before Mom noticed we were gone. It was only $5 from Norristown to the Thirtieth Street Station, round trip. The exhibit was in Fairmount Park, inside a makeshift shack set up beside the river, the interior walls painted black. A woman had outfitted several ballet dancers with microphones and asked them to dance. The recording of their breathing played, amplifying the tiny space with all those guttural huffs and sighs. We even heard joints cracking. We heard the thrusts of their bodies beating against air and space, minds catching muscle, saying *move*, saying *more*. There were no corresponding images; there was no music.

Eric left and waited for me outside, thinking the noises were too sexual. He didn't want to listen to that shit next to his sister.

"*Nasty*," he said in his faux-gangster drawl.

Truly, this was the stuff of birth, of original sin, of blood and atoms and energy. There were many narratives in this dark room, alongside the river, me in my city sweat. I was fascinated by the paradox of visual grace and apparent effortlessness with the grunts and groans of physical strain, an exertion I had previously associated with sex, or wrestling, or the delivery room in the hospital—but not ballet. It was maybe the first time I realized how two opposing truths could exist at the same time. Beauty and pain. Light and dark. Love and hate. That our father passed out on the floor was just a body on the floor. The battle was before.

So what of this other soundtrack, as two siblings rage inside a wan and forlorn motel room? What is going on inside their heads, beneath the shitty dialogue ("Fuck you, assface!"), the smack of mere matter? Where is *that* soundtrack? I'd like to layer it over a white background, poke around it like an insect. Is our grief written into our rage? Made smaller by the ferocity of baser emotions? If I could somehow transcribe the rhythm, turn it into language, maybe. Could I finger the phonetics? Sever the syllable that will drive us, finally, so far apart?

But it doesn't live here on the page. Our anger won't translate. So we will move in circles for years, colliding like meteors captured in the same orbit, both eventually sent off course.

One punch to the jaw. *Bam!* Even as I crumble to the ground, the pain searing up my jaw and settling sharply near my temples, I know there is justice here. And I mourn this moment like the final act in a play.

We won't fight this way again. That's what I finally understood in that second before he decked me in the face.

We don't know it yet, but the roles have been pre-prescribed, written into our DNA. What will become of Eric is barreling toward us, unstoppable. What we are more likely to understand now is that this cycle will not end with some apartment in the sky and thrice-weekly TV dinners. The second coming isn't coming. Our father is still in jail, our mother still earnest and struggling, the old escapes pointless. Our fighting costs energy we don't have the luxury of spending on such simple hurts.

Soon, I will start to worry about how often my brother gets high. I'll follow him around like a scorned lover, digging through drawers and reading private journals, handing out lectures even as I begin to snort Ritalin, at age sixteen, during my drive to school. I am bad at playing mother, and Eric will resent me for it. After so many vacations sleeping in the same room, we'll begin to lock our bedroom doors, each afraid of the other, still too close for our own good. Mom will begin to drink in earnest and develop her own pot habit. I will enter college and begin to drink compulsively, too, never satisfied. We'll spend years running away only to be yanked back in, as if attached to giant rubber bands fused to the home, soldered to our grief.

But now my brother and I are still sweaty and intimate, each of us gasping and dissecting the other's stricken face—studying the familiar bone structure, the close-set eyes, the swollen lips—when there is an authoritative knock on the motel room door. My brother rushes to me, uses the bottom of his T-shirt to wipe away the trickle of blood on my lip. We swing open the door and stand side by side. Our posture looks improbably rehearsed, the back of Eric's neck already blooming with blue whorls, my chin still sticky and pink. The cop is young, twenty-five or twenty-six, blond and stocky in her pressed, navy blue uniform, her bun beginning to unravel. Behind her the police car is idling. She doesn't plan to stay long.

I lean on Eric's shoulder casually. *Nothing happening here, Miss. Just getting the day started. Me and my bro.*

"Where are your parents?" she wants to know.

She wants to know where we belong, what we're doing here. We should know there were some noise complaints, some unhappy customers. *Why aren't we in school?* she wonders aloud. There is an expression on her face, pursed lips and disapproval, and I think I can read her mind.

She will leave. It is for the best. These kids still have their limbs, no? It's just noise, meaningless sound. Shit happens all the time, in places like this.

When Mom comes back to the motel room she is smiling, *buoyant*, a boat lined up and already paid for—"Half off 'cause I'm so cute!" We are already bundled up in oversized sweatshirts. I wear a scarf to disguise my purple jaw because *she needs our shit like a hole in the head.* The rain has not stopped, only slowed to a light drizzle, cold and clean. We will sit on this boat for hours, silent but for our breathing, hot gray puffs of steam like Morse code. We will be, for the moment, mollified by our own rhythms—bait, cast, reel, bait, cast, reel—our mother dangling a cigarette between her lips and fumbling with her line, occasionally calling out softly, "Here, fishy fishy, here, fishy."

PRETEND
WE
FELL
ASLEEP

MOST DAYS, CHARLENE and I ride our bikes down the big hill and through the woods to the creek, which is sometimes dry and sometimes not, but always full of fairies and the crumpled *Playboy* magazines that have been there since forever. Charlene lives next door, and so she is my best friend by default. She's ten now, which makes her two years older than me and in charge when we leave our yards, even to go across the street, even to the corner that's right there. We live in Philly's shadow, tucked under her poofy skirt. From the outside, our houses look the same, long and flat ranchers with bushes underneath the windows, which are yellow and wild like our daddies' mustaches. Inside, though, her house seems impossibly different. I like to trick myself by closing my eyes when we go through her front door, pretending it's my house, and then delighting when I open my eyes and see the TV that is much larger than I remembered, the couch suddenly navy instead of beige, the huge fish tank that wasn't there before bubbling in the corner. Best of all is her parents' room, though the door is always locked since the afternoon we walked in and her mom was sitting on her dad's lap ("Naked as they came," Charlene had explained. "'Cause they're in love."). They'd screamed, we'd screamed, and then we went out back to dig up worms from the garden.

Other days, we pick her mother's flowers and make bouquets, wrapping their stems in tinfoil and selling them on the corner for a dime apiece. Or else we leave our little brothers looking at the discarded *Playboy*s near the creek and run back home to tell. The fairies keep an eye on them, even when we do not. There are fairies in the trees and pictures of fairies in the magazines. You just have to look.

I like a game that involves secrets, a world that the grown-ups can no longer see. I have a vague idea that grown-ups have lost the ability to see magic. They are sad because they forgot. For example, at night I fly around my room. It has been so long since my mom has been that happy, she doesn't even remember, that's how long. I can't see the magic so much as I feel it, like all the plants and animals and rocks and things are thinking through me. Like I was born to do all the feeling for everything else. I also look really hard for any strange goings-on. Is that leaf moving on its own, or is it just the wind? And how many times have I seen that butterfly today? Should I follow her? My favorite book this year is *The Lion, the Witch, and the Wardrobe.* If I don't read it every night I can't sleep. I spend long hours curled up inside my closet, waiting for the door to open and the blackness of the regular world to fade away. If I sit very still I can feel the cold curl around my ankles and I hold my breath and wait.

Charlene's parents have a water bed, which makes me think they must be very rich.

"Welcome to the nineties," she tells me, as if that explains everything.

Before they locked the door to the bedroom, we would pretend their bed was an ocean and we were lost at sea with only one bag of Doritos to feed us until the pirates showed up, hauling us back to their island and loading our necks with heavy jewels from their treasure trove.

"We have to take our shirts off. Pirates don't wear shirts, only necklaces," Charlene would say, so we'd throw our T-shirts off the island and wave our chests around, the necklaces swishing back and forth and clinking like diamonds.

Now we play in Charlene's room, which is exactly where my room is next door, but her walls are pink and mine are white and she has see-through curtains like a princess. In my room I have plastic makeup and books and wool sweaters and penny loafers. I have stickers for being a good girl and a smart girl and a quiet girl. I have rewards for staying in my room and rewards for being sad when something bad happens, like when Dad comes home with a missing tooth or the coffee table crashes against the wall. I have rewards for having a dad who drinks too much and a mommy who works all the time. I like when people are pleased with me. I like rewards. I like being hugged and smiled at and cooed over. I crawl into laps. Sometimes, I want to be held so badly I shake like a hooked fish.

"You're the girl and I'm the boy," Charlene says.

I'm sick of being the girl because I know it means Charlene is going to boss me around, but I don't say anything because she's ten now. Also, she reads chapter books, which I guess is the trade-off when you lose the magic. For instance, she can't see fairies anymore, which is pretty sad because she's only ten. Ten is a dangerous age.

"Can I be the bartender this time?" I try.

"Girls aren't bartenders," she says, and even though my mom is a girl and a bartender, I keep quiet.

Charlene locks her bedroom door and pulls the see-through curtains closed. Outside, our little brothers are in the front yard pretending to be Ninja Turtles, and every ten minutes or so my brother will start to cry and her brother, Little Benny, will have to let him use his plastic sword or Eric will never shut up.

"Cowabunga!" I hear Eric scream, whacking the sword against the side of the house.

It's July, which means the ice cream man will drive down our street after dinner and we'll beg our parents for money and sometimes we'll get it and sometimes we won't. When we ask Charlene's dad, he calls us mooches and tells us to get a job, but then he usually forks it over. His jeans pockets are always jingly with change, which is another reason I'm pretty sure they're rich. That and the Nintendo.

"Whaddya having, honey?" Charlene asks as I stroll up to her nightstand.

"Hmm," I say. "Tequila Sunrise?"

This is the most grown-up drink we can think of, the drink her mom has sometimes while our dads drink cans of Budweiser. She takes her time pouring imaginary liquids into the Mickey Mouse mug that we always use for this purpose. She stirs with the handle of her hairbrush and then takes a sip, closing her eyes and moving her mouth around to test the flavor.

"Do you want a cherry?" she asks, setting the mug back on the nightstand.

I nod and she drops a scrunchy into my cup. I feel my cheeks getting warmer and I start to get squirmy. I know what comes next. Her bookshelves are filled with troll dolls with wild hair and I can't stand the way they're looking at me. Sometimes, if she's not paying attention, I'll shove one under her bed.

I will remember this game years later when I am having sex for the first time, thirteen and skinny and sprawled naked on a slick basement floor. I'm at my friend Katie's house, a dirty, dilapidated row home tucked between Third and Arch. Her parents are never home so Katie and I eat bags of sunflower seeds that we steal from the 7-Eleven and toss the trash on the floor. We smoke pot out of crooked tinfoil bowls and cajole neighborhood boys to buy us pizzas. We blast hip-hop from the one remaining speaker on her stepfather's stereo, stare at the ceiling, paint our toenails purple, and compare the bruises on our knobby, boyish legs. Katie is already having sex with Darren, her boyfriend of three weeks, and he has a friend who wants to fuck me—she is sure of it.

Katie is small and pretty with delicate features. Her left nostril is pierced with a tiny silver stud that looks like a wayward booger. While Katie has a full C-cup, disproportionate for her frame, I haven't even had my period yet.

"Perfect," she says. "You don't gotta worry about getting preggos or nothing."

Eventually, and for no good reason, I give in. I am thirteen and scared and bored and insecure and lonely and I let myself get banged on the floor of Katie O'Connor's basement, my tailbone pounding against concrete. The bruise is there for weeks. I don't even know his name, but I watch his black eyes widen when he grabs my hand and curls it around his penis, the first one I've seen in real life, and I know then I've made a mistake. It feels soft and hard at the same time and something inside me falls into a small hole just large enough to keep me steady. He groans with a voice like gravel and I hear Katie calling from the top of the stairs.

"Ooh girl, you havin' fun yet?" Katie giggles as Darren pulls her away by the waist, the door shutting and the last of the light slipping away. I hold on to the thought that this will be worth it in the end, that some part of this man-boy will never leave, even while I know I'll never see him again. When I can't hear Katie's voice anymore I think, *If I could just hear her voice, this will end.* I try to imagine my mother floating down the stairs. *If I could just hold her hand, crawl into her lap, burrow back inside of her and hide. If I could claw my way beneath the soft earth, eat worms, and curl up against tree roots and wait, I would. If this would just not be real.*

The dark boy bites hard on my small new breasts. I am buried and gone.

When it's over he holds me. I feel everything but safe, everything but what I need to feel. I remember Charlene, her warm arms and the cool quiet in her house, so different from mine. When she held me, we were the same girl with the same life and the same future. We lived on an island and we were pirates.

"SO," SAYS CHARLENE, "my shift is over."

She punches numbers into her calculator and pulls off her shirt. "Holy crapoli! It is so hot." She wipes at her flat, bare chest with her shirt and leans over the nightstand. "Do you want to come over to my place?"

"Sure!" I say too loudly. She shoots me a look that means shut up, so I do. I am a kid who likes to please and this will rarely serve me well.

"It's over here," she says, pulling me behind the curtains and pushing me down until I am lying flat on the floor.

She pulls up my shirt and hovers above me. I feel the heat from her belly and her hair tickles my neck. She has a round face and blue eyes that I wish were mine. We are both chubby and have big bangs that our mothers' curl under with a round brush and then feather like a plume, dousing our whole heads with aerosol hairspray until our bangs are stiff as peacocks. The boys have it worse. In the winter, they get their hair cut with bowls over their heads. In the summer, the mothers shave them clean. The rattails, though, are year-round.

"Ain't nobody touching my rattail," I heard Little Benny

say to Eric one day, a camouflage hunter's cap pulled down over his eyes.

"You have a *rat?*" Eric said.

"Rat*tail*, not *rat's tail*, dummy," he told him, yanking on my brother's hair so hard his head snapped back and he started to cry.

Little Benny is a bully, but Eric is a wuss. For years, he will befriend boys that make him cry. He is skinny and wimpy and bighearted and everything makes him cry. Dead squirrels make him cry. Yelling makes him cry. Sick people make him cry. I make him cry.

He is the only person I can control, which is one reason I love him best.

He turned to look at me in that second before the tears fell while Little Benny took off for the safety of his own backyard. His wrinkly little face broke my heart. I wanted to hug him and wipe away his tears, like our mother would.

"Suck it up," I said instead. I was practicing my pop-a-wheelie. "I can't do everything, for christsake and goddamnit."

Mom's working tonight, so Dad will make our favorite chicken pot pie from the box and we'll sit out back and count lightning bugs while he smokes. He won't have change for the ice cream truck so we don't bother asking. Eric doesn't like peas, so he flicks them into the grass one at a time. The neighbor's cat slinks out from under the porch and swipes at them with her paws until one lands on her neck and she goes crazy and takes off.

"I *like* peas," Eric insists, swinging his legs. "I just don't like to *eat* them."

Dad laughs so hard that I'm confused. He takes a long sip and wipes his mouth with the back of his sleeve, just like he's not supposed to.

"That's funny," I say.

"What is?" says Eric, stabbing a piece of chicken with his fork.

Dad is still laughing. His eyes are pink and watery. He slips off his work boots and stretches his long toes.

"That crazy cat," I say, shaking my head. "What a looney tune."

The backyard is getting dark. I eye a fat robin pecking the ground suspiciously and take note of the flying stars, the ones that earned their wings. I watch Dad go drowsy and I feel myself shrinking, small as an ant.

"Cowabunga!" Eric calls, launching another pea onto the grass.

"Let's say you forgot to wear underwear but I don't have any to lend you," Charlene says.

Her breath smells like candy and her hair smells like a swimming pool. My toes tingle and I start to squirm again, afraid that one of our brothers will look in the window and spot us here, skin to skin. This is Charlene's favorite game, and I like it because it makes her happy. I can't say why, but I think we'd be in trouble if our moms found us here, like when they found the boys looking at *Playboy*s down by the creek. Getting in trouble makes me feel like a squashed bug. I cry out for Mom to forgive me, *please forgive me*, even though all that crying only makes her madder, and don't I know that by now?

"Do you want me to kiss it?" Charlene asks.

I nod and she pulls down my pants and dryly kisses the round place between my legs. A single kiss. I go dizzy. I want to cry and ride my bike as fast as I can down a big hill at the same time. "There," she says, "now your turn." I kiss her in the same way in the same place, feeling frozen as a Popsicle, feeling the curtains fall over my back.

Years later, years during which we will move many towns apart and grow big and graduate from separate high schools and leave home, I will see Little Benny's picture on the news and learn how he killed a girl while driving drunk in the wrong lane, going in the wrong direction on the highway. And suddenly I'll realize it isn't Little Benny at all, but a stranger that, in truth, looks nothing like him, and I'll wonder at how quickly I'd judged him, like I'd been waiting for it all along. I'll worry about what that means about who I've become: a woman who assumes the worst.

I will find Charlene's wedding pictures on the Internet and marvel at how fat she has become, and how beautiful, and how her mother appeared small and shriveled beside her, both of them beaming. Months later a baby will appear, then another and another, and one will be called Little Benny Jr., after her father and her brother. I'll feel dried out and barren, even though I'll still secretly hope for kids of my own one day. I will wonder at my fear of mothering like a detached thing, some secret scar nobody else has to look at but me. I'll learn from a mutual friend that Charlene manages a local Genuardi's Supermarket and I'll suddenly recall a day when I was sixteen and walked into Genuardi's with a new friend I desperately wanted to impress. I saw Charlene bagging groceries and made up some excuse so we had to leave, afraid she would see me and call my name and I'd have to admit to this new friend that yes, we grew up together and yes, I had loved her unconditionally— this heavy girl in off-brand jeans and dirty sneakers and dark eyeliner like a superhero. I had been just a kid, and she was the last person I would ever love in that same, wide-eyed way.

"Now we hug," Charlene says.

We lie beneath the window with our arms around each other and listen to our brothers beat up bad guys. "*Hiya!*" they yell. Our clothes are strewn across the floor and the bar is closed. Somewhere, my daddy is on his third Budweiser and feeling better and better. My mom is fixing bologna sandwiches on white bread and ironing her work apron and smoking a cigarette all at the same time, trying not to let the ashes fall on the carpet. The ice cream truck is on the next street over playing "This Land Is Your Land" through the megaphone and Little Benny is whacking their old terrier, Jacko, for peeing on his "numb chucks."

"Let's pretend we fell asleep," Charlene whispers, pulling me closer and closer until I feel her breathing in my ear. It makes me sleepy. The music is getting louder and I hear the boys calling out to our mothers. I close my eyes and wait for the sound of the door swinging open.

THE
WHITEST
WINTER
LIGHT

I

JORDAN STICKS THE end of a safety pin into the pad of his thumb, saying that a moment of pain is the only relief from all of our past and all of our future. I laugh and grab his arm, pulling up his sleeve as if to check for scars. It's our first introduction and we are already huddled alone in a corner, the tulle of my dress clenched in his fist, the party devolving around us. I am cavalier. I laugh. He looks at me with resignation. I laugh so hard, until I start to cry.

We are both fifteen when we meet. I arrive at the party with a friend named Rachel who knows the hostess, a popular girl named Angel whom I have never spoken to before this night, though I've seen her around school. Rachel is my friend by accident. We met when we were both too young to be discriminate, and I think she's felt pity for me ever since. Though she's never said so, I think she has defended me to her friends in the past, and so I feel both grateful and pathetic whenever she calls. Since grade school, I have had a habit of befriending mostly foreign exchange students. The purpose of this is two-fold. For one, they don't know enough English to dislike me, or to fob me off for cooler friends. Also, I ern brownie points from my teachers for helping these students improve their English, which makes their job easier. And while I am too shy to be "teacher's pet," my very survival has always seemed dependent on the approval of adults.

Angel ushers us in and we spend many minutes in the hallway telling her how "cute" she looks and how "fantastic" her new shoes are. I follow the two girls down into the basement where a bunch of teenagers sit on old Victorian sofas. The walls are bare and the ceiling is low. The TV is on and I stand there awkwardly staring at the screen, pretending to be absorbed. I squint my eyes and tilt my head. I hope this expression conveys approachability and deep introspection, a chance for someone to break the spell and say, *Hey, what's up?* or *Whatchya watching?* But no one does. I don't like the idea of sparking conversation. The whole practice is lost on me; my mother's penchant for charm and wit skipped over me and settled on Eric, thirteen now, whom I hate, envy, and love in equal measure.

This is the popular crew, the kids I've been longing to know for as long as I can remember. Instead, I've managed to get by with a few "mid-level" friends. Not nerds, exactly, but not members of this higher echelon, either. I am reminded of this as Rachel introduces me to a handsome boy named Dave who looks at me curiously through a thick fringe of blond curls.

"Do you go to Wissahickon?" Dave asks. I've been in school with him since the second grade.

"I just moved here," I say, shrugging.

Dave takes a drag of his joint and hands me the tattered end, then jumps up from the sofa to change the station on the radio. The cherry burns a dull orange and then goes out by the time I get it to my lips. I roll the remnants between my thumb and forefinger and drop it to the ground. A girl I do not recognize is pouring shots of vodka into a variety of mugs and passing them around. I take a mug from Rachel. It has a picture of two gigantic cartoon breasts, the nipples distended and glistening. *Cream?* it reads.

I stick close to Rachel the entire night. Occasionally, Angel's mother yells for someone to *turn down the fucking radio* or *take the cigarettes outside.*

"Pot is okay," I hear Angel explaining to Dave. "The smell doesn't last so long."

By midnight I am drunk and warm, the chaos distilled into an even hum. The boy named Jordan is sitting next to me watching a TV show about a hamster, a *real, live* hamster, and his adventures in an overgrown backyard. The creature wears a tiny red helmet that Jordan finds *so freakin' adorable*. He laughs hysterically. Rachel laughs, too, but I can tell it is just an act. I don't find it that funny, either, just ridiculous. Jordan improvises dialogue in a high, squeaky voice and a bunch of girls begin to giggle with him.

I think this boy is beautiful and effeminate, delicate and self-conscious. I have never spoken to him before but have always wondered what it would be like to be his friend. He is close with all the most popular girls in school. Rachel tells me they fawn over him and let him dress them up for parties. They tend to him like a sick child when he gets too drunk, which is often, and defend him in front of their boyfriends. The boyfriends are beautiful, too, but not as bright as Jordan; they are confused and feel threatened by his effeminacy and the gentle way he braids their girlfriends' hair in our school hallways. These are girls Jordan's known his whole life; he's slept beside them at birthday parties, and at times when his parents needed him to go away. Their mothers have fed him, bathed him, and watched over him as their daughters dolled him up in their Sunday school dresses and matching pink sweaters.

For now, the party has died down and just the two of us remain on the basement floor. A girl named Sarah plops down beside us to tell me how her mother used to toss them in the same bathtub when they were young. She tells me that Jordan would shit every time the water was too warm, and so now she bathes only in cold water. She tells me how scared he became when the lights went out at night and how once, after they were a little older, she caught her brother masturbating beside the couch where Jordan slept, her brother's pink prick hovering over the soles of Jordan's bare feet.

"Did he jizz on you?" Sarah asks him. "Gross."

We are silent as the car climbs the steep, cobbled hill in West Philadelphia where Jordan's father was last seen. He takes hard drags on one of my cigarettes and picks at the black ringlets of hair on top of his head.

"Your head looks like an octopus," I say, and he blows smoke in my face.

Jordan needs money—for food or drugs, or his own goddamn cigarettes, that's for sure. The tip regarding his father's whereabouts came from his aunt, whom Jordan had stayed with briefly when he was fifteen and his mother had first kicked him out of her condo. It was a good thing, though, because management would evict Jordan's mother just a few weeks later and, the aunt had told him, she was naked and high when the manager came to serve the notice. *So high she threw a frozen hot dog at him.* She left all of their stuff behind, including Jordan's broken bed frame and the cat, Snickers. Jordan does not care to know where his mother went and assumes that she is staying with one of her drug dealers. For a while, we would sneak into the condo through a basement window to give the cat fresh food and water. Snickers hid every time we came in, which forced us to clamber over boxes of clothes and unused exercise equipment to find him. We tried to avoid eye contact with the mannequin heads, Styrofoam models his mother had once used to hold the wigs she styled for beauty school. The heads, white and stoic, lay helter-skelter on a metal shelf like dejected parts in a doll factory. After a few months, we stopped showing up and the condo sold. Nobody knows what became of its contents, or the cat.

When we find Jordan's father he is in front of an open garage, slouched in an old metal wheelchair like a lifeless marionette, a dirty, white puff of a dog curling in and out of the rusty wheels. His pink scalp is chapped and flaking and he is fiddling with something on his lap. A few old men sit in folding metal chairs inside the garage. They smoke and pass around a bottle of brown liquor. They watch a television set that is rigged up in a corner on top of some cardboard boxes. A younger man, maybe in his fifties, stands against a wall and rubs his forehead back and forth, back and forth against the coarse concrete. I stay in the car while Jordan gets out and moves toward his father. I notice that his walk is stiff and awkward, a feigned masculinity. His father hands him a twenty-dollar bill that Jordan stuffs into his jeans pocket. He turns around and rushes to the car, gets into the passenger seat, and slams the door.

"Go," he says, sliding another of my cigarettes from the pack.

How many nights have we spent in this basement? A hundred? More?

Angel's mom is crazy. Everybody knows that. So is Angel, for that matter, all of five feet nothing, her tiny, olive feet jammed into shimmery stiletto heels, shoes built for a steadier gal—but here we are. Angel is like a wind-up toy, fueled by booze and prescription pills and countless joints, wholly reliant on boys who will pick her up from the floor and toss her little body over their shoulders. They take her to bed. Her black skirt slips high over her hips, delicate as wishbones. And her ass, compact in the requisite G-string, is warm against their cheeks.

We all use her, this sixteen-year-old girl, for her house and her drugs and the entertainment she provides. Her mother's negligence is a boon, her father's absence merely a convenience.

Some say he died a couple of years ago. Others say he moved to Las Vegas and runs a casino. We don't feel bad; few of us have fathers anymore. We like to watch as the self-awareness drains from her eyes. It is so tangible, that moment, composure puddling around her ankles like a silk slip. Jordan passes her the joint and she inhales greedily, desperately.

"Jesus, Angel," he says, and snatches the television remote from her lap.

Her boyfriend, Rick, watches her and laughs, her pretty face scrunched in concentration, tossed back toward the ceiling. Her eyes are closed. She digs the thin heels of her shoes into the floor, drawing black lines through a collection of ash.

"All right, baby. Damn!" he scolds, pushing her into the couch cushions and stealing the joint. The gesture is neither affectionate nor aggressive. I know from experience that Angel can snap in an instant; she is prone to scream wildly when it is least expected. This is part of the fun. Jordan looks at me conspiratorially.

"I love you, Peanut," he mouths.

He disappears upstairs for a while. I hear him talking with Angel's mom about pierogis, and then I hear her offer him a plate. He has a look that makes women want to feed him. Rick and Angel have settled into the corner of the sofa, his arms around her as she dozes on his shoulder, the strap of her dress dangling, revealing the edges of a deep-crimson bra. It surprises me to see them behaving so intimately; they look so young. Last night, a blonde from a neighboring school had shown up at Angel's door looking for Rick. Before he could get to her,

Angel had spit in the girl's face and somehow torn the front of her shirt. The night ended with Angel yelling curses at the back of Rick's rusted, yellow Volkswagen and Angel's mother screaming from her bedroom window, "Shut the fuck up! Just shut the fuck up, Angel!" But now, Rick kisses her neck and she wiggles her small fingers into the pocket of his jeans.

"Crazy bitch," Rick whispers tenderly.

I get up to retrieve my school bag from the corner of the room where I'd dropped it hours ago. I don't have any boy-friends and I am beginning to worry that I never will. I still scribble the names of my crushes inside school notebooks and ignore them in person as a matter of course. I know my aloof-ness to be a symptom of shyness, but secretly I hope that it con-veys some measure of mystery and seduction. So far, it hasn't.

Rick carries Angel upstairs. I sit and wait for Jordan to return, sipping on bad red wine and finishing up some homework. My mother thinks that I am here to tutor Angel, and sometimes I stay overnight. She doesn't actually believe it, but we play the game anyway. It's a precarious arrangement that works for now. She's spent so many years dealing with a drunk husband, she hasn't the energy to worry over me. I'm the good egg, and that's that. In the meantime, Eric has been diagnosed with ADHD and is getting in trouble at school. Homework is a nightly battle. He smokes pot all day, every day. She works constantly, selling real estate alongside her mother, and she does well. We get by. I keep my shit together, and that seems to be enough for now.

When we are not at Angel's, Jordan and I are at my house. He rarely goes home anymore. We sleep side by side in my bed, and by the time we get there we are too stoned to talk properly, preferring to tell each other fairytales involving young Robert Plant and a desert at night. Campfires blooming in the dirt. A fifth of whiskey. In our dreams, we sing like Stevie Nicks. We dance wildly like Janis Joplin. Once, in the middle of the night, I stuck my hand up the back of his T-shirt and felt the cold knobs of his spine. He wasn't asleep like I'd thought and he rolled away slowly and sighed.

Jordan comes downstairs with a second helping of pierogis in a glass bowl. He places three blue Ritalin in front of me on the coffee table, though I know there are more in his pocket. He is an unabashed thief. He licks the gravy from his spoon, dries it on his jeans, and begins to crush one pill into a fine powder. "Wait!" I say. "Take your time." He ignores me now, because he knows I am as addicted to the process as to the drug itself. I am hooked on the anticipation, the crunch of the pill, the swirl of blue sand, and the careful way Jordan builds the lines, like distant desert mountains. We take turns with a rolled-up dollar bill. The smell of money, that particular synthetic burn, will years later still elicit a Pavlovian shudder and a cold ache in my jaw.

We swig back glasses of wine and light cigarettes. "Let's take a walk," I say.

"I can't move," says Jordan. "I mean, I just want to be right here, with you."

We sit quietly, smoking, and I feel my thoughts begin to trip over one another, my heart racing. I watch the old flip clock clicking through those arbitrary numbers, and it seems so loud, that clicking, like Ms. Gregori's heavy black heels echoing down the hallway. She was our ninth-grade English teacher who smoked incessantly and wore the same clunky black heels every day, even in the heat of late spring.

"Doesn't that clock sound like Ms. Gregori stomping down the hallway? Like when it's empty, you know, when everyone's in class and you're going to the bathroom or something? And then she's just there, all of a sudden. You know how she's always just *there, everywhere*, all at once, with that notebook and all that red hair? I think she might be psychic, or like a witch or something. Do you know what I mean?" I ask. "How she's always *there*, wherever you are."

Jordan reaches over and covers the clock with a blanket. It goes silent, which we soon realize is not the same as stopping time.

"I love her," I say.

"She hates me," says Jordan. "They all hate me." He takes another gulp of his wine, and then refills our mugs from the giant bottle of Carlo Rossi, the one with the glass handle that Angel's mom bought for us earlier that day.

"Do me a favor," she had said to Jordan. "Don't steal Angel's Ritalin tonight. I can't afford to keep refilling that girl's prescription."

"Mrs. Farley," he said from the front seat of her car, "it was an experiment, that one time. I'm sorry it happened," he said, as if it were something beyond his control.

I said nothing, the mute accomplice, the silent partner. Nobody expects anything bad from me. My own mother, least of all. Then Jordan had leaned over and gently kissed Angel's mom on the cheek, and pulled her pale hair from the rubber band that had held it away from her face.

"There," he had said. "You are so beautiful."

Around 2:30 AM, we hear footsteps on the kitchen floor above us. We hide our notebooks under the sofa and feign sleep, clumped together on the floor, our feet tangled under a yellow blanket. The heater clicks on and then there is the rush of water pouring through old pipes. I turn off the lamp. I yawn despite the pounding in my chest, despite the water crashing through a terrible quiet and the cold tears on my arm that make me shiver.

"Why are you crying?" I whisper to Jordan.

"Shut up," he says, as Angel storms across the room and tears away our blanket.

"What the fuck?" she yells. "Are you guys, like, making out?"

She turns on the lamp. The room spins into focus. Our mugs of wine sit next to us on the floor. She looks like a lion, her skin yellow in the artificial light, all that curly hair sticking straight up in the air. She is wearing a Boyz II Men T-shirt and that stupid purple thong. Jordan starts to laugh. We were not, of course, making out, but instead writing poems in our spiral notebooks—serious poems that we imagine ironic and witty, but are really just sarcastic.

"Angel!" he says. "Your hair is trying to escape from your head!"

"Where's Rick?" she says. "Where'd he go?" She turns around and surveys the room as if he might be hiding in a corner, or crouched behind the giant television set.

"Lost him again, have you?" says Jordan, but by now she is gone, turning off our light with the main switch by the staircase, all the way over there.

"All the way over there," I say.

"What?"

"All the way over there. The light. It's all the way over there." Jordan sighs and wipes at his face.

"I think I can do it," he says gravely, "if you set up another line."

"This is not good," I say, because that's what I always say. Jordan gets up and heads toward the stairs.

"Pean, it's fine," he says, because that's what he always says. "Read me the last stanza."

We read our shitty poems and drink our shitty wine. We talk about our parents and how awful their drug problems are, and yet, how much we love them still, and we try to make sense of it all because now would be the time to do that. We think aloud, *Now would be the time to do that one thing.*

"Let's take a walk," I say.

"Pean," he says, crying again. "I like girls *and* boys."

This crying is really getting to me. Here I am, and that sun, which isn't here yet, could show up at any moment unannounced, as it tends to do. The world will start up its endless, painstaking rotations, and all the people will get out of bed. Rested and cogent, they will slip into their hot showers and later drink coffee with cream and head out into their driveways to start the car, to go to work or school, and here I haven't even managed to finish my homework. I can't even finish my homework and the night has come to an end. Or it will end. And then there's everything else to contend with.

"Pean," I say, because we are both "Pean," short for "Peanut," short for brevity's sake, for the sake of time. "Pean, is that the sun? Please tell me that's not the sun."

"That's not the sun, Pean." Jordan covers us with the blanket again. I throw my sock at the wall, which is covered in planks of synthetic wood. "Pean, did you hear what I said? Did you hear me, Pean?"

"If you would just stop *crying*," I say, "we could have a rational conversation for once."

I am panicking. The television suddenly flickers and black lines begin to fall down the face of the screen before it all turns to fuzz. It's muted, but still.

"Oh my God," I say. "Do you know what that means? It means it's late, really late, and soon the sun will come up. I can't bear to see the sun. God, I hate that fucking sun."

Jordan constructs another line on the table top.

"We should go to an Al-Anon meeting!" he says suddenly, as if this would solve all of our problems.

We've been to meetings before, doted on by forsaken wives clustering around us like mother bears. We couldn't find our "higher power." That was the problem. A heavyset woman named Sheryl once told us that if we couldn't imagine anything larger than ourselves, we've got some real ego issues.

"Well, you're certainly larger than us," Jordan had said, dropping the end of his cigarette into one of the Styrofoam cups set out for this purpose.

It all seemed like faulty logic to me, but I didn't say so aloud, and I think we both spent the better part of a month more insecure than ever. When my brother and I were kids and our father had started drinking again in earnest, my mother had us go to Alateen meetings. Even then we were cynical, willfully refusing to hold hands for the Lord's Prayer. Eventually, the group leader asked our mother to send us to a different meeting, perhaps coupled with some quality talk therapy.

"I know your kids are Jewish, Ms. Nelson," she said, "but the Lord's Prayer is for *everyone*, no matter what your higher power may be."

Well, that pissed her off, because when it came to religion, our family was about as faithful as a used-car salesman, so she knew we'd been giving this lady a line.

"I'm not going to any more Al-Anon meetings," I say. "I would like, however, to go for a fucking walk. I have to get out of this basement before the sun comes up."

This seems imperative to me now, as if I could somehow outfox the sun simply by getting there first. Jordan takes a final sip of wine before tucking into the fetal position and covering himself with the yellow blanket.

"I think I like girls *and* boys, Pean," he says.

"No, you don't, Pean," I say. "You just like boys."

I sit on the floor by the side of the couch and dig my toes into the curls of Berber carpeting. I'm scared to be left alone here, but I know that once he closes his eyes he's gone, and that will be that.

"I guess you're right," he says, closing his eyes. "You're probably right."

I lie down beside him and try to slow my racing heart by matching my breaths with the rise and fall of his ribcage. The whitest winter light travels through a small rectangular window near the ceiling. In this light, I think I see the pores on the curve of his earlobe and feel the pinch of a silver safety pin still lodged in the pad of his thumb.

II

"Somebody found his bag," my mother says when I pick up the phone.

I'm in my junior year at the University of New Hampshire and I'm late for class. My cell reception fades in and out. I watch girls in miniskirts flounce past me, their white legs glowing like heat lamps in the spring sun. Some boys play Frisbee on the lawn, barefoot and bare-chested. I light a cigarette as I listen and try to look casual. Jordan's disappearing acts are not new. My mother has grown accustomed to his sudden absences and has even received similar phone calls about the bag. Some Good Samaritan finds his wallet inside and locates my mother's number. The first time, we panicked. We don't do that anymore. We have to function, my mother says. Now, I imagine Jordan in Philly with a lover late at night. They are both drunk and stumbling and Jordan's blue eyes are red and wet like hard candy. Maybe there is an argument between them. Maybe Jordan storms off, or jumps in a cab, only to realize later that he doesn't have any money, that the bag has become as irksome as the rest of his responsibilities, and when he trips over the curb and skins his knee and drops his bag, he'll leave it lying in the gutter like so much trash, the green corduroy swelling with yesterday's rain.

My mother retrieves his bag from Good Samaritan number three, a retired police officer, and Jordan shows up at her door a few days later. He is strung out and toeing the zinnia plant in front of her porch. She yells. He cries. She makes him a sandwich and puts him to bed. He calls my phone that night but I stopped answering months before. I am done saving him, and pretty soon so is my mother. We aren't the only ones. He has other women, moonlighters who provide the occasional ride or free meal. As he gets older, he turns increasingly to men for that comfort, but he abandons them before they can abandon him. That's how the game works, he tells me.

I imagine Jordan does not sleep well that night in Eric's old room. I imagine he sweats out the booze between the sheets and cries all alone with only the entrails of a coke binge to keep him company. I imagine he thinks about last night's boy, his vodka kisses and the mercurial currents of spent lust. I imagine him biting the pillow and then thrashing his legs like he does when he is tired but cannot sleep. I believe he decides, quite suddenly, that the best way out of the guilt is to just disappear.

My mother recalls leaving for work around ten and hearing him softly snoring behind Eric's bedroom door. When she comes home, he is gone again. This time he never comes back. No more phone calls, no more recovered bags. His old boyfriend, Michael, will call me much later to say that he and Jordan have broken up, that he could no longer take the theatrics, the well-deep depressions, the finely tuned addictions, and the inevitable disappearances and infidelities that went along with them.

"I came home one night and he was using a paring knife to cut a star into his abdomen, yakked out of his mind." Michael told me.

Two years earlier, though, when I went off to college for the first time, things had been different. Together, Jordan and my mother had been devoted fans of reality television, late-night bowling, and antidepressants. Jordan would listen to her "realtor voice" as she negotiated sales over the telephone, and then mimic her assertive tone in his voicemail messages. *Jessica, it's Jordan. Listen, I need you to call me back a.s.a.p. regarding those contracts. We're not budging without an inspection.* We pretended it was practice for the real world.

When I returned home for winter break freshman year, I found Jordan and my mother sitting on the couch, smoking and watching the ten o'clock news. Jordan was living in Eric's room then. He'd spent so many nights there during our senior year of high school and then, one day, he just never left. My brother's belongings had been stuffed inside a hall closet, the oversized T-shirts, tattered textbooks, dirty socks, and crumpled tinfoil bowls. The gangster posters remained on the walls, though, and the mattress still stank of stale cigarette smoke.

Eric was seventeen and living in a drug rehab for juveniles, a court-mandated placement after a year of truancy and dirty piss tests and then seven disastrous months living in Las Vegas with our uncle, Mom's only brother. Out of desperation, perhaps, my mother had hoped that Eric would straighten out under the guidance of a "positive male influence." It didn't work. When my uncle finally returned home after delivering my brother to the airport for an early-morning flight back to Philadelphia, he discovered his safe wide open and nearly empty. All that remained were his youngest daughter's birth certificate and a sheaf of old business documents. Exactly how much money my brother and his friends managed to get away with remains a point of contention, but it is generally estimated at around the $10,000 mark.

But Jordan was better company anyway, as attached to me as a new puppy and prone to muttering witticisms from the side of his mouth. There was wine on the table and he was curled up and leaning one cheek on his left palm, his fingers twisting in and out of his newly blackened hair and a cigarette held high in the other hand. He smoked like a coquettish film star from the thirties, taking long drags and then whipping the hand away and holding the burning cigarette above his shoulder, a burdensome thing. There was great flourish to most of his gestures, but he was a terrible hugger, reaching around with one thin arm and patting my shoulder blade with the fiery hand, the blue smoke lapping at my hair. He felt even smaller than before, bird-boned and fragile. I wanted to squeeze him hard and kiss his *keppie*, as my mother would say. Yiddish for "head."

"You're kissin' the wrong keppie, Pean," he said, laughing.

We hugged and he went back to the couch, plopping down dramatically and sighing, as if exhausted.

"Welcome home, Pean," he said.

"Oh, yes," said my mother, "welcome home!"

They looked like a couple of loafing teenagers, both of them in raggedy T-shirts and sweat pants I knew were once mine.

"Our prodigal returns," Jordan said, beaming at my mother.

"Oh, yes," she said, "our little college girl."

She'd been trying to get Jordan enough financial aid to attend community college. It was a lot of paperwork and then there was the question of his missing parents. It was a question without answers. My mother had walked him through the process of acquiring free, need-based healthcare and he'd finally found a job at a nearby beauty parlor washing hair and sweeping up after haircuts. My mother dropped him off and picked him up every day. It was the longest he'd ever held on to a job, five months, and he felt good about it. He'd even tried to give my mother some rent once, a couple hundred bucks, but she'd surprised us both by turning it down. He said he might want to try beauty school again, if he could just save some money.

After my mother went to bed, we rolled up some of her weed and sat out back, as we'd done so many times before. The dog came, too, and darted into the bushes, dirt catching in the wind and flying back at us.

"This is her new thing," Jordan said, rubbing at his face. "That and wiping her ass all over the carpet."

We sat silently for a while, watching the dog bury her toy in the ground, then unbury it, then bury it again. She worked inside the fog of her own breath and the midnight gray of winter stasis.

"I'm gonna bury your feet," he said, "so you can't go back."

I thought about this for a long time. There was the sound of the dog's scraping and the crackle of the joint as we inhaled. I reached over to pick at some dead skin hanging from his bottom lip.

"What if it rains?"

"I guess I'll get you one of those hats with a built-in umbrella."

"That would be nice of you," I said, my head suddenly light.

"Oh well, then, forget it."

My feet itched, but I didn't feel like taking off my shoes. I sensed the hairs on my arm standing up from the cold while the warm smoke rushed into my lungs. The dog barked and the whole world shook. We talked about his new boyfriend, a freckled boy named Michael whom he'd met at his last job waiting tables. Jordan was fired for drinking during his shift, but the two had exchanged numbers and they'd been dating ever since.

"Mostly we do blow and watch Björk videos," he said dreamily.

"My feet itch," I said.

"Yeah, he's pretty great."

Jordan licked his fingers and put out the joint, sticking the roach into his cigarette pack. The dog had finished with her ritual and made herself comfortable atop Jordan's feet, panting softly and nibbling between her toes. He reached down to rub the dog behind her ears and she looked up at him gratefully, all love.

Jordan disappeared only once during our senior year of high school when I was still living at home. He wasn't there when I went to pick him up from work. We didn't know where he was for five days. My mother and I paced the house together, both in pajamas, the dog running circles around our legs. It was winter and very cold. I scraped the frost from my car windows and drove aimlessly around the city. On the sixth day, I woke up early. My nose tickled. I came to slowly and blinked into Jordan's big blue eyes, his nose pressed against mine. He was straddling me in the bed and smiled broadly when I awoke, kissing me on each cheek and laughing. My room was filled with the sugary blue of early dawn. I wanted to slap his face, but all I could do was hug him and pull him beneath the blankets where it was warm.

"I met someone special," he whispered.

"You're special," I said. "Like eats-the-paste special."

He nibbled my shoulder.

"I'm too excited to sleep," he said.

"Shh," I breathed, a new exhaustion already pulling me under.

Outside, winter birds were calling out from the shadows. I heard a great gust of wind hit my window and felt his breath against my neck. Within months, I'd be off to college. *We find what sustains us*, a professor will tell me later, *and if we are very careful, or very lucky, we do not lose it.*

Those last few months of high school were like a dream. It was 2002. In March of that year, I learned that I had not been accepted into any colleges outside of Pennsylvania. My father died on April 4th. Eric picked up where our father left off then, entering the endless cycle between rehabs, halfway houses, jails, and relapses.

Jordan started to steal things: money, clothes, cigarettes. When we fought, he whined and begged for forgiveness, which drove me crazy. "I'm such an asshole," he said over and over. I agreed, but we made up because I was too tired not to. He called Angel often and went over there just to schmooze some Ritalin. I'd stopped joining in, but only because I couldn't stand coming down from the stuff, my whole psyche shattering at my feet. I didn't talk to anyone. I turned off my phone.

Jordan and I spent three months in my mother's basement, idly peeling glow-in-the-dark pot leaves from the walls and trying to convince ourselves that we were going somewhere. Occasionally, one of us would climb upstairs to make toast and, at some point in mid-April, I filled out a bunch of last-minute applications to colleges in New England. Meanwhile, my mother gave up any pretense of ignoring our pot habit and started joining us for bong sessions in the basement. It was like family dinner, but without dinner. Instead, we ate only things that could be peeled or buttered. Jordan went to parties and called me to pick him up at odd hours of the morning. I didn't really mind. I was sleeping in snapshots.

In September, I climbed out of the basement, packed my bags, and drove to New Hampshire with my mother. As we

crossed the bridge into Durham, I saw white sailboats bobbing innocuously in the bay and a pair of sleek silver birds dive
into the water like bullets, one and then the other. Yes, I felt
I would finish what my father could not. Yes, I had never felt
more his child. I was grieving, and those boats, this place—it
was the closest I could get. It was home before I'd ever arrived.
"This is it," I told my mother. "So long for now."

My mother laughed and giddily slapped my knee. I smelled
pine needles and, inexplicably, Tabasco sauce. I watched the
herons placidly drift beneath the bridge and a woman shaking
a blanket over the stern of an old wooden boat. The sky faded
to black. We saw the stars then, so far from the familiar city
lights. Nobody honked, even when we forgot to go.

"Almost there," said my mother, "and just in time."

III

Rachel calls on a sunny day in April. She's recently finished
college and moved back home, sort of, to a place called Mana-
yunk just outside the city limits. I am busy fishing the remnants of a taco dinner from deep in the kitchen drain. My hair
is wet from the shower and I have to keep putting the phone
down to wipe it away from my face. She tells me that Jordan is
in town for a few days, that an old beau paid for a round-trip
plane ticket from Austin. And yet, he showed up at *her* apartment and is now sleeping on *her* sofa and leaving swathes of
liquid foundation on *her* bathroom counter. He is also eating

her food and helping himself to the *good* wine she received as a Christmas present. I am living in New York now, just north of Manhattan in Yonkers, and recently started graduate school at Sarah Lawrence College. *But still*, I think, *he could have called.*

"He's so skinny, I can see his black little heart," she says.

I don't ask why she's letting him stay in the first place. I know I'd probably do the same. And then, as if she is reading my mind, she says, "I'm not driving him to the airport. That is where I draw the line."

Later, I work a fine, dark topsoil into my garden while wearing new magenta gloves. I get tomato seeds from my landlord. I sit back in the sun, chewing and squinting into the sky. My arms feel tight and strong. There is the smell of cilantro, like soap, and the buzz of the cicadas on the tree trunks. I sip a glass of ice water and imagine swimming. It is a Sunday, which means that tonight I will make a salmon dinner and wash my hair and read a book and fall asleep early. I am working toward a Masters of Fine Arts in writing, a degree I suspect will not help me find a job and I'm certain will sink me $40,000 in debt. Right now, I don't care. Everything is white. I am hooked to an IV of words and ideas and I am fading, faded, and gone. In the morning, I will drink coffee with cream and go to class and this is just fine. I am taking care of my body, my nerves, my feathery brain. I am saying *I forgive you*, this missive to myself.

Two days later, Rachel calls me back. She is on her way home from the airport.

I sit outside on a lawn chair, remembering. I am searching for usable scraps, memories of what was good and pure between

Jordan and me, but find only the metallic ends of a winter drive. Or else, the rusted edges of those endless nights in that basement, where we drank wine and snorted a friend's Ritalin until we felt our teenaged, suburban angst change to a tentative self-assurance. While I wait, another day turns into night and I am that much further away from the girl and the boy who loved each other once, for a few painful years, and now do not know each other at all. And this, too, I know, is just typical, and yet we never thought we were typical at all. I would like to write a letter to that boy, to tell him that I am no longer a young girl and all is forgiven—if not, as they say, forgotten. I do not trust my memories and so I wait, and in that time the memories continue to swell and change shape.

The last time I see Jordan he is tending bar at a club called Woody's, which is tucked into an alleyway near the Delaware River, the *gayborhood*, we called it, south of the Avenue of the Arts. If we stayed within a six-block radius, we could pretend the whole world was a carnival, and love and sex and rainbows were free and in abundance, an edible candy land like Willy Wonka's factory. We used to come here when we were young and bored. We liked to watch the boys float around the dance floor. Bisexual angels, all glitter and pomp. There were moments of transcendence here, too, when the neon light struck a silver crescent on the cheekbone of some man-boy, his face upturned and his arms thrown back and slick with sweat. One night we met a man who dressed in tunics and spoke in pastels. "He speaks in pastels!" we told each other, on account of the drugs, but also because of the way the strobe lights reflected off his tongue. He wore his hair in two long black braids that slid over his shoulders like ribbons.

We loved him instantly, though for different reasons, and followed him everywhere that night, hiding behind the felt partitions and whispering fantasies that again involved desert fires and a guitar, this modern-day Indian chief our own personal deity now, some munificent daddy sent to show us the way. If Jordan's fantasy involved the lure of sexual tutelage, mine was just the opposite. I was after the press of the paternal, some utterly chaste discipline I sought out everywhere, anywhere. The truth is, we were vulnerable in those days, our minds all sweet and custardy from too many drugs, overwhelmed by the theater of the senses. We made a good show of normalcy when we needed to, but most of the time we retreated into our own basement novella and held on for dear life.

IT IS LATE June when I enter the dark tunnel that leads into Woody's Bar, and I am a woman on a mission. It has been three years since I've seen my friend. My mother and I have come from a restaurant down the street. I've just graduated from college and returned to Philadelphia for a few weeks. We are celebrating my impending move to New York and also the sale of a big property my mother had listed for months. Real estate has been painfully slow, but business is starting to pick up and she is hopeful for the first time in a long time. I know this not because she tells me, but because she is laughing at my jokes and her eyes flutter girlishly in the candlelight.

When I first see Woody's familiar red sign, I am startled. I almost forgot about it. I'd heard rumors that Jordan recently started bartending here and we decide to stop in. We are not— we agree to this on penalty of death—out to save him again.

We find him at the upstairs bar and watch for a while before he sees us. He moves quickly and confidently, no longer a boy agog. I see that he feels more secure, rooted and blossomed, but with the same nervous energy shuddering just below the surface. My mother holds my hand and I know we look like lesbians, given the context. There is a man watching Jordan make drinks. He leans on the bar, discreetly running a gaze down Jordan's white neck, flat chest, and narrow waist, his short, thin legs wrapped tightly in pale denim. The man yells to be heard above the music.

"This drink is weak, sweetie!" he says.

Jordan snatches the drink from across the bar. I imagine the chilled glass feeling good on his chapped lips. He swallows the rest of the lime-green concoction and grins.

"No," says Jordan, "it's just fine."

The man says nothing. He watches Jordan bend for an-other bottle of Stoli, then lays a five-dollar bill on the counter and begins to write something at the top. Jordan pockets the money without noticing.

"Well, he's alive," my mother says.

We are huddled in a corner. For a moment, I think we are going to turn around, to scurry down those graffiti-laden stairs and step back out into the alley, relieved. This boy breaks hearts and I am afraid.

The music is heavy techno, the sort of thing that my mother hates. She once told us that club music sounds like shrapnel hitting a rainbow. At the time, we laughed so hard Jordan spewed ginger ale from his nose. Now, I think she may have had a point. It feels like the music is trying to beat itself out inside me, to exhaust an energy I cannot contain. I haven't been in a club for years. I feel world-weary and I'm only twenty-two. I look over and Jordan has spotted us, two ridiculous mother-hens tittering in a corner. He turns suddenly, like he hasn't seen us, and begins to needlessly align the liquor bottles, turning them so that their labels face out. I see his hands shake. I see him wipe his nose with the bar towel. I see him muss with his hair, which is in a mohawk now, and take a deep breath. I know what these gestures signify—he isn't done with the coke.

"I've been meaning to call," he says as we approach the bar.

"Oh, please," my mother says. "Make me a martini, will you?"

Jordan fills a silver shaker with ice, retrieves the bottle of Grey Goose from its spot on the shelf, and pours for a long while. She must look older to him now. She's put on weight; the freckles have grown darker and more pronounced. Lines have begun to wend their way across her face. I don't know how I look. My hair is dark and swept up instead of long and blond. My clothes have gotten more tailored, I suppose, and less tight. I try to do a credible impression of a model citizen, the professional young woman, but I suspect he sees through all that. He pours me a glass of Malbec and leans over to kiss me on the cheek.

"How's Eric?" he says.

"Back at home. Stable for the moment."

"You graduated?"

"Yes, sir."

A man yells, his long-blond-haired head poking up from behind my mother's shoulder, "What's on draft?"

Jordan pours a Budweiser and hands it to him.

"Take this on the house," he says. "All we got tonight, honey."

The man winks, hands him a twenty. My mother looks around, as if just now realizing that she's out of her element. She begins to stare. I believe she thinks this is good for Jordan, better for him than her blue-shuttered suburban home, quiet neighborhood, and golden retriever. *Nothing wrong with learning a little self-reliance.* I know she's not angry, even though she misses him, misses smoking cigarettes on the back porch and giggling like kids.

Jordan works around us, answering questions in mumbles. Mom sits patiently, running her fingernail over breaks in the wood, turning her head to watch men kiss one another, intrigued. Jordan gives her pretzels and she nibbles through the whole bowl.

"Did I get fat?" asks Jordan. But my mother doesn't hear. "Mom! Did I get fatter?"

She looks him up and down. "Thinner, if that's possible," she says.

"You guys look great," Jordan says. He bites at his thumb. "Do you hate me?"

"I'm too old to hate," my mother says.

"Another drink?" We nod.

He serves a few more drinks to other customers, sliding down the length of the bar, flipping bottles, pouring mini shots into plastic cups and swallowing them down. Men tip him generously. He shoves the bills into his back pocket, winks, and pulses his hips to the last beats of music. The strobe lights have settled down and, just like prom, the DJ puts on one last slow dance. Some people get up from their tables, bleary-eyed and groping for their partners. A few drag queens crowd around a window with their cigarettes, talking quietly and blowing smoke rings that hang in the air like halos. An older man remains perpetually at the end of the bar, nursing a whiskey and speaking in tongues. His bottom lip is bleeding and I watch Jordan dampen a napkin and give it to him, pointing to the spot. There is a gold and phallic chandelier dangling in the center of the dance floor. It projects tiny dots of color that alight on the skin of the dancers, on their damp cheeks and arms. A spot of blue plays inside a young man's belly button. I've been sitting too long and move out into the revelers with my glass of wine. I hear Jordan laugh as one of the queens takes my hand and twirls me around, then pulls me close to her. She smells like citrus and cloves, like the shed I used to play in at my grandparents' house when I was a kid, the bags of peat moss piled high like a castle wall. A plume of purple feathers sticks out from the bodice of her dress and they tickle my cheek as she dips me back in her arms. We do a little do-si-do. Look at Mom, all smiles and good intentions, her hands folded in front of her as if in prayer. Beyond her is my old friend, clasped tightly in someone's arms, his head on the man's shoulder. They dance slowly, an impromptu love affair, a moment's pardon from all that has passed and all that is to come.

THE
PRESENT

The present is an invisible electron; its lightning path traced faintly on a blackened screen is fleet, and fleeing, and gone . . . No, the point is that not only does time fly and do we die, but that in these reckless conditions we live at all, and are vouchsafed, for the duration of certain inexplicable moments, to know it.

—Annie Dillard, *Pilgrim at Tinker Creek*

I

1998.

In the beginning, he does not remember switches and directions. To blow his nose. To wash. Irving gives up napkins; he wipes his mouth with his sleeve. He pees on the floor. He farts in public, but louder than before. He chews with his mouth open. At this Helen hollers and we cringe and laugh, laugh at age and its particular idiosyncrasies.

When is the beginning?

When I still measure time by cracks in the sidewalk.

How long?

From here to the crack that looks like a volcano and back again.

On my bike or running fast?

On my bike, and as if I don't have to get off to walk it across the street.

Nights at Mom's office are longer than that even, after she quits bartending and starts selling real estate with our maternal grandmother, Helen. It is like going to the crack with the dandelions at the top of the hill and back again *three hundred times*. We're here almost every night. It's called Tornetta Realty Corp., and we like all the men named Tornetta, especially Frank, who looks like a ship's captain with his white beard and cigar. Eric and I are supposed to do our homework in the break room upstairs, around the corner from the office Mom shares with Helen, but instead we creep downstairs where the lights are off and all the desks are empty. We play hide-and-go-seek, but Eric always hides in the cubicle with the Hershey's Kisses, so it isn't much fun after a while. I stuff all the neon-colored paper clips into my backpack and use other people's highlighters to decorate my shoes. If the secretary, old Barb, is still there, she'll take us for rides in her little blue convertible while we play with the radio and she smokes long skinny cigarettes and talks about being alone.

Sometimes our grandfather, Irving, picks us up and takes us to Burger King, or else he makes bananas 'n' cream and I fetch the Tastykakes from the freezer in the garage. This is when kids don't eat organic anything, before he forgets how to talk. This is when the world is no bigger than the space between home and the creek bed, and phone numbers don't have area codes. When a stray Barbie leg still occasionally pops up through the couch cushions. When I can work myself into a panic just by thinking about death.

How long?

Forever.

Never coming back?

Never, never, never.

This is when Lawrence Welk comes on at eight and Irving uses the remote as a baton while we yodel like the Lennon Sisters. When the three of us whine every time Mom and Helen start talking real estate.

No more real estate! we cry out.

No more kvetching! they holler back.

Helen calls Irving "Mr. G" and he calls her "Mrs. G." This is when they are feeling fond.

"What's for big D, Mrs. G?" he asks.

He is one of those guys who retired early and can take off his thumb and see zoo animals in your ears. He makes ugly faces when Mrs. G turns her back and I giggle years after I no longer find it funny. He is as dependable as Saturday morning cartoons. He falls asleep in his Barcalounger ten minutes after he turns on the TV. He sneaks Reese's Pieces from a cabinet under the bar and slips them into our cupped hands when the women aren't looking. Half his retirement is spent grocery shopping and walking the mall before it opens at nine. He looks like a giraffe when he walks, lumbering, all limbs. He travels only when Helen makes him, and even then it's only to the Jersey Shore, where he can pace the boardwalk and keep an eye on the grandkids flailing recklessly in the surf.

Their house is on the corner of Red Rowen Lane, across from the elementary school where I used to chase boys, where my mother used to chase boys, where she once caught one by the scruff and said, "How about a kiss, big boy?" It's a split-level home, built during the housing boom of the sixties, with the Philadelphia skyline squinting in the distance. Until a few years ago, the furniture was still wrapped in plastic. The dining room is a celebration of Japanese tchotchkes and the floors are covered in plush beige carpet. Helen collects Swarovski crystal figurines. She gets them as gifts for every birthday and on every night of every Chanukah. To me, they are the most delicate and expensive gifts ever and I covet their tiny ruby eyes, the glinting sapphire stems and leaves. Glass seahorses and teddy bears line the windowsills, and hearts and pink roses fill a mirrored display case that hangs collecting dust in the living room.

Their house is the most beautiful place in the world, and the safest. We sleep over every time our daddy goes "off the nut," though we don't yet know what that means exactly. It is big and cozy and every room is its own universe. I like the master bathroom best, with the mirrors on every wall that let you see back into forever. A million little mes. As in, there's me a hundred years ago, tiny as can be, wearing the same dumb purple shirt. And then there's the shower like a Whac-A-Mole game; water spews from any one of nine different nozzles, and you never know which one will turn on next.

When we spend the night, Irving lets us fall asleep watching *The Mary Tyler Moore Show*. In the morning, he paces the hallway in front of the guest room and pokes his head in the doorway every few minutes, checking to see if we are awake, if we are breathing. Through half-closed eyes, I see his face flash blue and red in the television light.

"Let them sleep, Irv!" I hear Helen call up the stairs, but he never listens.

I squeeze my eyes shut and pray to fall back under, lonely for my dreams. During breakfast, Eric sits on his lap and I trace the scabs on the top of his bald head. I am going through a rare skinny phase and he pinches my ribs woefully, shaking his head. His hands are as big as baseball gloves. If he were my father, I'd be fat and safe, like a caterpillar in her cocoon. Later, in the laundry room, my mother trims the thin strip of white hair that rings his scalp from ear to ear and I sit on the washing machine, watching. It's been her job for as long as I can remember and I think of myself as her apprentice. She dances as she works, drumming on the top of his head and snapping along to a song no one else can hear. She clips his nose hairs with the trimmer and he sneezes and swats her away like a cranky child.

"Hold still," she says, sitting on his knees and cupping his chin with her other hand.

"Hold still," I say from the washing machine.

II

In India, there is a tale of memory and a man. The man, a yogi, is lost, and in his wanderings he falls in love with a queen. He is besotted by her beauty, so enamored that he follows her to her kingdom and stays—forgetting all about his convictions of understanding and of purity. Finally, on a journey into the spirit world, a devoted disciple learns of his master's enslavement and becomes convinced that this memory loss will cause the yogi's death. Desperate to cure his loved one of this spell of amnesia, the student scours the Book of Fates in the realm of death and determinedly erases his master's name from the list of the dead. With little time remaining, the student then flees to find his master in Ceylon and, disguised as a dancing girl, sings and dances until the afflicted man is finally returned to himself—his memory restored and his faith and identity replenished.

Science tells a different story of memory, though it is no less enrapturing, no less mystical. It starts with our origins in the ocean and it reveals a reliance on the salts of such tremulous beginnings. The neurons that become so tangled in an Alzheimer's patient are what allow memories to be developed in the first place. They receive signals from outside the body, a tiny shiver of charge. And yet, it is the balance of salts within these tiny neural threads that cause the charges, and the firings back and forth. In their own complex and symphonic way, the neurons create a summary report of their activity. This summary is what we feel as experience—and memory.

III

2007.
This is the end of a life: a man in a box. The lid is ajar and an electric light beats down on his forehead. This man is old and

bald and thin, thinner now than ever before. He wears a dated
suit, the one with the pale-blue satin vest that he wore to two
daughters' weddings. His hands are crossed over his stomach.
There is a thick coat of liquid foundation over the deep purple
bruises that spread from his bulbous knuckles to his child-
sized wrists. His face is painted on, the earlobes swollen stiff
with embalming fluid. There are six white hairs sprouting
from his left ear. His chin bears a wash of new, spiky white
stubble. There are thirty-one people here. I counted. Twice.

IV

In the end, he does not remember being thirteen, waking at
dawn and tossing a heavy wool blanket to the floor. He does
not remember the sweat and the impatient bleating of the
milkman's horse or the clanking of bottles on the porch below
his window. His mother calling him for breakfast in Yiddish,
iberbaysn, her voice loud through the thin walls of their narrow
row home in Philadelphia. He does not remember the leather
belt he stole from the bedroom of a heavyset neighborhood
pal named Frank. Chiseling the extra notch through its thick
skin with his father's pen knife, his pants drooping anyhow.
He does not remember when he began to introduce himself as
Frank to the local Italian storeowners because he was certain
they weren't hiring him because he was a Jew. At sixteen, can-
ning soup at the Campbell's Soup factory across the river in
New Jersey. Giving all his wages to his father. Relinquishing

their home to the bank anyhow, for the sake of $300. He does not remember losing his virginity to a neighborhood hooker and the bruises on her thighs. His tiny apartment in South Philadelphia that he shared with his first wife, Stella, who drank gin and tonics until morning and beat on his chest with her red fists. Finding out she was sleeping with his best friend.

He pretended not to remember the two children from their marriage. (And I never learn to reconcile these two ideas of him—the devoted father, the absent one.)

He does not remember working thirty years on the Philadelphia naval base. The black soot that he picked from underneath his nails every night. The upholstery samples that he carried door-to-door in the evenings, their ornate brocades like Braille only he could read. He does not remember Yiddish or the Torah. He does not remember how to wash a dish or how to hold a fork. How to speak. Being poor. Being middle class. How to write a check. How to fix an engine. How to wipe his own ass. How to make love. A family. How to call for them. Taste. Time.

V

2007.

This is a Jewish funeral in Northeast Philadelphia at a place called Goldstein's on the side of teeming, litter-strewn Highway Seventy-Six. The place is gray and neon and inundated with sharp angles and low ceilings and a disharmony of colors. An aunt has called in her rabbi for the service because Irving has not been to synagogue in thirty years.

There are also a handful of grandchildren here, of whom I am the eldest. Eric is beside me in a yellow jumpsuit and handcuffs. We are sitting in the second row behind the "principal mourners"—Helen and her children: our mother, two aunts, and an uncle. Notoriously creative, my brother and I have draped a gray suit jacket over his shoulders and I hold his hands. My wrist shields the handcuffs. My brother's keepers lean against a wall at the end of our pew. One of these officers is chewing gum and blowing tiny bubbles that he hooks back into his mouth with his tongue. I sneak him dirty looks in between greetings from old family friends. I resolve to keep an eye on *them* for a change.

Two days earlier, Goldstein had showed us around the casket room. He looks like a used-car salesman. He is middle-aged and fat and has a full head of gleaming white hair that looks waxed into place. A thick mustache is perched above his swollen lips. He'd said things like "and because your mother's such a sweetheart, I'll throw in an annual power washing for the stone there, free of charge!"

The casket room was dimmed, a series of stoic spotlights showcasing each open box, highlighting the delicate folds and tucks of plush satin lining, baby blue and angelic white. Goldstein led us through the maze, running his fat fingers over gleaming bronze handles, demonstrating their magnificent heft and polish, their leak-proof locking mechanisms. Most of the caskets looked overwhelmingly large on their pedestals. Some were child-sized. I stood behind my two aunts, my mother, and my grandmother and watched as Goldstein gently, dangerously toured us through our grief. He stopped occasionally to finger seals and talk numbers. When we were unresponsive he grew restless, excited even, a thin wash of sweat on his face. I sat on a bench while Goldstein went to get us some water. I watched as he handed my mother a plastic cup, slipped an arm around her waist, and led her to an immense mahogany number, all sexy curves and heavy, phallic handles. On clearance now, $7,999.

Irving Gordon, a lover of deals of all kinds, a penny pincher fitting the worst of Jewish stereotypes, would have balked at such a frivolous expense, cocking his thumb toward the precarious construction of two-by-fours in the corner before nodding his assent and retrieving his checkbook. Even this economy model, with its fraying rope handles and complete lack of any kind of leak-proofing, will run the savvy buyer a cool grand. I am sure Irving would have found irony in his last shameful scamming, the sum of his pittance from Veterans Affairs buried along with him. In this way and in others, we are wholly divorced from our heritage, eager to exchange the Jewish mandate that we bury our dead in a plain pine box for the easy comfort of knowing we gave him satin. Nonetheless, his women finally settled on a mid-range, Aurora brand box in "devotion silver" with adjustable handles, though sans adjustable headrest. This, Helen decided, will suffice.

In the end, Irving had grown so thin that Goldstein will have to pin his suit tenderly behind the shoulder blades, discreetly at the small of the back. He paints my grandfather's face with smooth peach foundation and presses earthen rouge into the hollows of his cheeks. It is a surprisingly tactful reproduction, a tender, vain dressing of the corpse—horrific and exactly right.

After the funeral, the mourners disperse. The rabbi goes home. My brother must go back to jail. His keepers rap their thumbs on the side of an open van door, waiting. I slip Eric a cigarette and the cop nods and looks away, squinting into a light rain. Eric takes quick drags by bending down toward his hands, which, in addition to being shackled together, are linked to a heavy leather belt cinched tight around his skinny hips. His dark hair is cut too close to his scalp, light fuzz beginning to develop on his chin and jawline. He is twenty years old.

The first offense is theft, though many others will follow—a wildly colorful rap sheet—but the disease that makes him do such things is just an infant now, just an infant throwing its peas. Right now, Eric and I are more distraught by the way he is attending this funeral than we are by the death itself. Death, this time around, is a small grace, we think, though we don't say so aloud. When I look at my mother, her face puffy with grief, I feel a love so large I can barely breathe, and beneath that is something so dark and ugly I am only just able to translate it into words—something like, *At least you had your father for fifty-one years; we buried our father years ago.* Grief tinged with envy. This thought is so terrifying and cruel I won't be able to look her in the eyes for hours, only hold her close.

"Can't they just let him come to the cemetery?" Helen asks loudly, for the benefit of the two officers.

They are growing impatient now. The big one unlocks a door and nods at Eric.

"All right, let's go," he says. Eric takes one last drag from his cigarette and flicks it into a puddle of mud.

"Now, wait a minute," says Helen.

"Lady, you think this is a joke?" says one of the cops.

My mother and I gasp. We can't believe someone would speak to Helen like that. Sweet, grieving, *elderly* Helen. My brother clenches his jaw. The women glare. The man senses his misstep and backs down some.

"All right, kid, let's go. Give Grandma a hug and then get in the goddamn van, okay?"

Helen clutches onto her grandson's bony shoulders, pulling him into her neck. I see Eric pull away at the waist, trying to keep his handcuffs from touching the swell of her stomach. She pulls him in harder. He gets into the van and they drive away.

VI

I hate to consider that we are merely a sum of our memories—those which our minds choose to hold on to, those which we cannot help but let go, despite ourselves. That's all we have, I think, that's all we are. These memories, however, are far from fixed. They shift with the changing tides of the water on our brains, the dubious salt of mere matter. A cold northeast wind, perhaps. Who can say for sure? Each remembering is different, each successive dredging more unreliable than the last. Our brains recreate (as a function of self-defense, or self-sabotage maybe) a slightly larger hand, a slightly longer hug, a steeper walk, a harder ache, a toothier smile, a smaller child. This time the joy was more acute, the eruption deeper, the color red not blue. This time it sounded from a distance; this time it felt more like this.

And the present? The present may be no more than three to twelve seconds, according to William James and a modest experiment at the turn of the last century—a compulsive attempt to "quantify" the present. Three to twelve seconds. A sip of wine. A violinist's high C. A soccer ball drawing a white arc through the buggy air. Shifting the car into park. Failing to recognize your house key. Your own yellow toes. Samuel Johnson wrote that "the bright edge of consciousness moves quickly, and the present, after all, is in perpetual motion, a precarious ledge. It leaves us as soon as it arrives, ceases to be present before its presence is well perceived, and is only known to have existed at all by the effects which it leaves behind." A heron beats his great wings against a southern-bound fog, lifts its long neck toward a hidden lolling sun, a dense rotating rudder raised to catch a breeze and shift direction. He leaves only a trail of memory in his wake. He is gone before he has even arrived. In *Pilgrim at Tinker Creek*, Annie Dillard recounts an experience, a moment of pure presence, in which she is simply petting a dog. As she is "patting the puppy," however, she is suddenly gripped with the exquisite pleasure of the now, an overwhelming awareness of her own consciousness and its inexorable end. "This is it," she writes, "right now, the present, this empty gas station, here, this western wind, this tang of coffee on the tongue, and I am patting the puppy, I am watching the mountain." Then it is over.

I feel this level of consciousness rarely. A moment of such clarity and self-awareness, the sense of brick and brain and the wood beneath my bare feet, of skin and wind and the rush, rush of cars passing and time tumbling over its shoe-laces. The fly dancing down a windowpane, the robotic, slow-motion twitching of its legs when it lands on my wrist. That particular itch.

VII

2007.

Day one of Shiva. My mother and I wake late. She smokes a cigarette and we drink good coffee. There is a message on her answering machine from Helen.

"Susan, it's your mother. I just wanted to *remind* you to wear your black mourner's button because the rabbi will be here tonight and I think, well, I think he's kind of *checking*."

My mother on one couch, me on the other, we stare each other in the face and laugh. Then we cry. The two dogs hear the commotion and come bounding into the living room. They are panting and their tails are going and they trip over each other's legs trying to get to my mother. They career into her shins and topple onto her bare feet. They are looking at her anxiously, waiting to know just what is going on. We have to get our shit together.

"Get your shit together," my mother says.

And so, finally, we do. We finish our coffees and I take our cups into the kitchen. I hear my mother light another cigarette and speak softly to her dogs.

"It's okay," she tells them. "This is okay."

My mother and I arrive at Helen's house. She's forgotten her mourner's button after all. In truth, I think she lost it. Helen's house is still empty, except for the rabbi, and we start unwrapping trays of bagels and fishes and sliced red onions.

"Actually," our new rabbi says, "Shiva is traditionally seven days but we just don't have time for that anymore. People still have to make a living—even rabbis."

I am instructed to contemplate the cyclical nature of life and death as I grab a poppy seed bagel from a basket and slather on some scallion cream cheese; the round foods that are always served during Shiva are meant to drive this concept home. After a couple of bites I decide I do my best contemplating with a glass of wine, so this is just going to have to wait.

I am under the impression that this is a time for the "principal mourners" to rest, to reflect, to eat a lot. Yet Helen is still scurrying around the house, draping old dish towels over the mirrors in order to keep out the spirits and discourage vanity (but mostly, I think, to show off in front of the rabbi). When we finally get hold of her, her eyes are wide and panicky, her full face drawn together into a fierce look of concern.

"Sit," we say, but she never listens, either, just like Mr. G. She *has* to clean the powder room toilet before company arrives.

At sundown in Helen's house we all stand in a circle and say a prayer we do not know in a language we cannot understand. Helen's face is serious as the rabbi sings the lilting Hebrew and the rest of us stumble through the English translation in what appear to be purple Prayer Books for Dummies. I am sitting on the steps with my little cousins, four and six and seven years of age, their newly acquired Hebrew in perfect unison. I am struck by the conviction of their Hebrew school educations (an education I never had), and I say a silent prayer for my brother and for the cousins, too—a prayer that this faith will be more sustaining for them than the one I am struggling to erect for myself.

But it feels good to stand with family, friends, and some strangers, and say a prayer of something, out loud, together. We say it for him.

VIII

2006.
We are visiting Irving at the nursing home, the whole family. The staff is throwing a hula party where we all dress up in grass skirts and bright leis to dance to quick beats and loose rhythms—the nurses and the families, and his favorite gal, nurse Jane, with the green smock and the ice cream spoon. I

dance in front of Irving. I am lip-synching to Jimmy Buffet and Irving is thinking *oy gevalt, crazy girl, what's her name*—or is it just flashes of color sweeping across his blank, blue eyes? Eric has dressed him in an old Eagles' jersey. We are devoted football fans. The shirt is baggy on Irving and reaches his knees, but Eric likes this and says, "Poppop's chillin'."

Eric is eighteen now, a popular high school senior. He uses vocabulary that he learns from rap songs and tries it out on Irving, who is inspecting his new shirt. Mom and I dance while Helen chats up the nurses. Mom is a better dancer than I am and she knows it. She has more rhythm. She does a slow tango with herself, one hand on her stomach and the other arm draped over an imaginary partner. An old man in a military jacket wants to know if I've seen Agnes. A nurse starts to feed him a virgin margarita through a straw and he sucks hard and smiles and licks his lips.

"How's my love, Mr. G?" Helen says, covering her husband's hand with hers.

I keep dancing and reach toward him, bringing my palms to rest on his cheeks. Beneath the blare of that old radio, the silence still stings. Rather than suffer the indignities of his mistakes, it seemed Irving made the decision not to speak at all. It happened early on and almost overnight. I pull at his cheeks, then press them together to purse his lips. *Smack*— a kiss—and I swear he's smiled; wondered at that nose, that freckle; said my name. We are dancing to a restoration that will never come, swaying to a lost identity. But for now, he is slumped over the wheelchair handlebars and drooling onto his lap, holding my hand, and watching his family dance this dance, this dance, this dance, this dance.

How long?

Three to twelve seconds. There to here.

A SECOND
OF
STARTLING
REGRET

TWO TINY MOUTHS emerge from a bed of hay and sticks and yellowed leaves, brown beaks chomping on desiccated air. Black eyes blink frantically. The new hawks swallow the dust that rises in plumes from a dry nest as they beat their wings and scuttle their webbed feet. Their mother tucks her chin to her breast and nibbles at an insect burrowing into her feathers. She lifts her head to the sky. A cloud stutters in front of the midday sun and there is a second of shadow and chill and the yellow electric tinge of danger. She is completely still.

A great wind moves suddenly and the big hawk shudders and heaves, her long neck expanding and contracting, her bird-boned shoulders pressing back tightly. Her head moves in rapid, twitching circles. Stiffened wings beat quickly against her swollen flank and the two young hawks caw wildly in anticipation of food, careening forward and over one another, mouths ajar. With one final downward thrust, the mother hawk inserts her curved beak into a waiting mouth and deposits a churned, milky stream of food. The little bird chokes and spits its breakfast to the ground.

　　　　　　　　　　　　　*

My mother sifts through an oversized pocketbook. She digs past a fat wallet stuffed with credit cards, a smattering of wrinkled business cards (her own and others), ChapSticks and lighters and loose tobacco and empty pill bottles. She pulls out the soft, green corduroy case that contains her glass pipe and a big bag of good pot.

We sit on her back patio at dusk: Eric, Mom, and me. This is where we land whenever I am in limbo, between moves or jobs or schools; we collect like tumbleweeds into the hollow of the backyard. We hunker down like weatherworn old men, sated for a moment with warm food and red wine and an old familiarity that settles the heart. We drink and tell stories and smoke cigarettes. This night, in 2007, is August warm and the sky is beginning to darken, heavy on our shoulders like a navy blanket. My brother takes a long pull from the bowl, prodding expertly at the hot orange bud with the corner of his red lighter. His brow is furrowed, and as he exhales there is a moment when his face softens and his eyes roll back and he is no longer twenty-one but six, or five, or three, before he has learned the plain facts of death and disease and the self-sabotaging brain.

I have just returned from a summer spent studying at Oxford after three weeks of traveling alone in Scotland and so

I start to tell them about midnight on the Isle of Skye, off the western coast of Scotland, which in June means wet fog and violet skies and loud pubs that pulsate with the heavy trill of local fiddlers. Neither Eric nor my mother has ever left the States so I am being especially specific, as if I could transfer the memories directly, as if I could give them away like postcards.

"Yeah, that's cool," Eric says. "That's real cool. I've been on a trip, too—a real trip. To the psycho doctor. And I am now the proud owner of a bipolar diagnosis!" He pauses to light the bowl. "The guy said it like I won something." Eric lowers his chin, exhales, and clears his throat. "'And with your family history . . . Yep, you've got it, kid!'"

"Well, we can see how he's taken to the art of self-medicating," says my mother.

The three of us shrug and nod and take long sips from stemmed glasses. I haven't lived at home for nearly six years. I've never lived in this house, actually, the farmhouse that looms behind us, our mother's dream home, which she bought the year after I left for college when the real estate bubble had not yet burst, when she was still making money. The farm-house blocks the noise of traffic and the bushes obscure the strip mall that has taken over the land that once comprised the farm's acreage, many decades ago. On nights like this, when the parking lot has gone still and the day's business has ended, we are able to pretend the safety lights still burning at Genuardi's Supermarket are pieces of the moon and the deer crunching over dead leaves are after fallen stalks of corn, and not the rubbish overflowing the dumpsters. Illusions like these are what keep us coming back together; we are practiced in the art of pretend. We are able to convince ourselves that drinking and smoking are incidental, and not part of the fabric of our family, of the shared anxieties that causes us, each to varying degrees, to feel so dissatisfied with our own brain chemistry. We are trying to return to a place of innocence, to the time before, when Mother could still keep us safe.

We keep trying, but morning light is unforgiving.

■

In Oxford, I am studying Pre-Raphaelitism and Decadence, which means I am doing a lot of thinking about parlors and flagellation and Japanese kimono prints. But I am also thinking about the uncanny. What Freud defines as "that class of frightening that leads back to what is known of old and long familiar." *Unheimlich*, in German. A word that means unfamiliar, *not home*, but also unconcealed, what is revealed. A word that moves in circles until it finally coincides with its opposite, *heimlich*, belonging to the house. *Home*. But it would be incorrect to assume that only the unfamiliar is frightening. The uncanny is the red swell of recognition, the buried obsession, the glossy vaginal folds, the former *heim*. Yes, this *is* terrifying, we decide, and off we run.

After three months, I am travel-weary and punch-drunk on paint, lost in Rossetti's blues and the pink tongues of Persephone's pomegranate seeds. I am leaving Oxford's museums thinking that the whole world is *now in HD satellite picture!*

like a big joke, a commercial's refrain having somehow mixed in my mind with the clarity of those images. This happens sometimes when I've been left to my own devices for a while, roaming foreign countries alone like some empty, vaporous disciple, rootless and hungry.

Between loneliness and exhilaration is a bit of madness, too. I have a trick up my sleeve. I am able to convince myself that I am unattached—come from nowhere, headed nowhere—without a home. Here, I subsist on worship, but my mother's God never came for me. Instead of spirits and symbols, I kneel to the crooked trees and the yellow ageless finch, the silver and sallow riverbed that winds wanly through an old village, which is ashen and crumbling and useless. Every strange face is suddenly familiar, as if from long ago, and every train heads in the right direction.

When I call my mother from a pay phone she tells me to get my shit together and hangs up. It's a good idea, I think, except that in the morning I tripped over my own feet, landing chest first on the stone steps of the Bodleian Library, my left breast now swollen to twice its normal cup size. Purple-red flesh capsizing over the edges of a black lace bra. I wonder why I missed out on my mother's level-headedness, which gene got pinched.

In truth, I tell her, I might be too far gone.

At night we gather in the Trinity College dining hall for a supper of fish and chips and something vaguely broccoli-ish, all soaked in buttery Hollandaise sauce. The warm white room pulses like a fever—hot skin of the eager, the underdressed. Grim portraits line the walls; under the accusing scowls of long-dead deans and bishops and moneyed benefactors, we sit and twitch and shift. We pull at thin dresses or khaki shorts and discreetly wipe away the sweat beneath our knees.

I eat slowly and leave. The courtyard is empty and the last light is glowing phosphorescent on the stone walkway. From another courtyard I can hear the hum of voices, the occasional crescendo of laughter. A door opens; music escapes and silver clatters on a wooden floor. As I head toward the pub to join my friends for a pint, I see two baby hawks huddled beneath the archway that leads from Front Quad into Chapel Quad. I step past them cautiously. They have the soft, pillowy down of the newly born and their small round faces are tucked into gray-white tufts which stand on end as if windblown, grasping for heat. And despite the warm summer air these chicks are shivering, eyes closed, silent. I look around for a mother and see none. I find my friend Maggie in the bar and she says not to worry, even if the birds fell from their nest the mother will be along to feed them eventually. This sounds right to me, but when we return through the archway a few hours later they are still there, swaying, knock-kneed, their breathing shallow.

■

"All right, clean up," says our mother. The lights in the parking lot are blinking now and it is becoming harder to pretend that they are anything but what they are.

"Why do you always do that?" I ask.

"Do what?"

"Order us to clean up dinner like we're still kids." Eric begins to gather plates. "As if we're not going to do it anyway. Besides, it's Eric's turn. I did it last time."

But she is older now. We all are. I notice her slower gait, the slight hesitation when she rises from a chair, the unsteady first steps. The constant Marlboro burning like an extra appendage. We are not a team anymore. "What we are" is the problem in general, since what we are is only a vestige of where we have been, the clunky manifestation of an abstract set of memories, and even these are made up, an experiment. When we come together, it is partly an effort to cling to something shared from long ago, even while we know these memories are as varied and variable as the people we have become. The shadow of the familiar is still just a shadow, and yet we'll never stop hunting it down. It is the only thing that makes us feel real.

"Go get Mommy another glass of wine," she orders.

This is the point Eric and I know too well, the time of evening we have come to dread. She will begin to slur and stroke our heads too lovingly. She will ride a conversation to unintended heights and then watch the thoughts tumble over an unforeseen precipice, bewildered.

We bring the bottle. We have learned to just bring the bottle.

And so we all settle back into our chairs. We watch the dogs wander through the yard, the gray one clawing new holes in the ground, the yellow retriever stamping at fireflies and then bellowing into the night. The azalea bushes next to the patio are shrunken from a late-summer heat wave, while the untended roses, having long since given up, lie flat atop the dirt. It is near midnight and a couple of cars sit idling in the parking lot behind the fence and the bushes, up to no good. I feel tired and heavy-lidded. There is dew collecting on the glass table and sweat in the crooks of my elbows. For a while, the only sound is the hum of the cicadas or the electric buzz of the telephone wires; I can't tell which. This is the sound I'd been hearing all summer right before I fell asleep, though it had been the sound of my dreams taking shape, the sound of letting go. Many nights, I was afraid. I was further away from my family than I had ever been and I thought it meant I had relinquished some measure of control over our collective fate. Sleep was a devastating reminder, a small death, and it made breathing difficult. I fought it. I paced the hostel lobbies and empty dining rooms in Scotland. I sat in the window of my dorm room in Oxford, watching the lines of people swerve around the late-night french fry stand. I'd thought to bear witness was to stave off disaster and by leaving I had done irreparable damage, not just to the three of us as individuals, but to the vital organ that bound us and kept us safe. I didn't yet understand that we were like conjoined triplets. What happens after surgery is yet unknown, but we've no shot if we mean to keep on sharing the same heart.

"Okay, Jess, tell another 'ye old weary world traveler' story," says Eric.

"Oh no, forget it," I say, exhausted.

"No, really," he says, filling my glass with wine.

"Please," says Mom. Her words are thick now, eyes red and dangerous. There is always this moment, when the wine and pot reach the point of saturation and reveal a second of startling regret. She is ready for bed.

I want to tell them a lovely little story about green and undulating landscapes, about skies soft as cotton and faces old as dirt.

I want to say, "We'll go, let's go."

I want to tell them about Vernon Lee and Freud and the uncanny, about sheep and whiskey and Scottish folk songs. Could I explain that to return home is not a return from the uncanny, but a return to it? Who would I be if I said that I don't belong here, don't belong anywhere?

Or . . .

But what could I possibly say of churches?

Instead, I tell them this:

For three days, we kept a steady vigil over the baby hawks. I have never witnessed a death so slow. I was there when it finally happened. The two birds, covered in flies, finally stumbled apart and moved toward opposite corners of the courtyard. Their progress was hindered because they could not see, their eyelids closed and swarmed by the flies. Every so often one would lose its balance and collapse sideways onto the stone, or else reel forward and back like a drunk, clumps of feathers scattering in its wake like tattered, shiftless cerements. I did not smash their heads with rocks. I did not slice their throats with a kitchen knife. I only watched as they floundered to the rose beds and clawed beneath the brush, biding time in separate charnels, a wonder to the worms.

FALL

A BLACKFACE EWE stumbles in a northern wind. She is high in the mountains on the Isle of Skye—a small but sturdy chip of land long ago cast from the great shoulders of the mainland. The ewe works a clump of grass against a toothless upper jaw as she leans her heavy, woolen flank against a rock for balance. As the wind tumbles down the cliff she recognizes the distant bleating of lambs, her own and others, but rambles further up the mountainside, chewing as she goes. Further down, some members of the flock sense her distance and look up from their grazing. They recognize her absence and are unnerved. *How far she has wandered.* A young ram lowers his head to scrape his horns in a patch of shorn grass and wet mud, blinking into the rain. An older ram takes off in the direction of the wayward ewe, but stops short to gum a silver stalk of asphodel bent over the cold water of a shallow stream.

This stream slices its way down the mountainside and collects under the wooden bridge where we are gathered, belly-down and hovering over the water, our faces submerged for seven, six, five more seconds. My arms shake as I try to hold myself up. Graeme is counting down from somewhere, laughing as he reminds us of the promise of eternal youth and beauty, the Scottish fable that has us facedown in this frigid water, eye to eye with a tiny world of undulating lichen, microscopic fairies tucked into their folds. I remember now why I prefer to travel by myself; even lonely, even hungry, even weatherworn and aimless. I stay this side of sea level.

Five years before I journey alone to Scotland, my father sits in his mother's attic in the Philadelphia suburbs and takes shots of Gordon's vodka from the bottle. Her new townhouse is in a town called Worcester, thirty miles north of where I grew up, on the top of a hill so high it is always windblown and cloud-covered, like a castle in a fairytale. He reads a book about a seagull that shares his name: Jonathan. He folds his T-shirts and places calls to my cell phone, none of which I answer. Two flights down, my grandmother Cynthia sips tea and mutters softly to herself as she turns off lights and locks doors, her legs swollen with her latest bout of sciatica. It is so painful she has to grip the banister with both hands and drag her weight slowly up the stairs. She is unhappy with a son living upstairs again, but grateful for what she believes to be his new sobriety, the catalogues from community colleges collecting on her dining room table, and the working stove that he has rigged together with an ell bracket and a spool of fishing wire. Jon is forty-four years old and has spent most of this time drunk, drugged, and drained, in a constant battle with his own brain.

He is a tired, uneager student.

The group wipes at red cheeks and ambles toward the idling gray bus: eleven Korean college students and me. I've latched on to the tail end of their three-week tour after introducing myself to Graeme in the living room of my Skye hostel. He agrees to let me onto his tour bus for their last day on the island only after I promise to teach his group a "quality American drinking game" when we return. Eventually, I'll teach them Flip Cup in the dim kitchen of the rakish hostel—a quiet affair that quickly digresses into a scene from a "quality American dance club," our guide and his Korean students doing the Macarena on the kitchen floor. I'll slip outside and smoke cigarettes and sip amber whiskey from a safe distance on the other side of the window, hips thrusting involuntarily to a hard beat on an empty island under a dusky hollow sky.

But first, the gray bus must wind its way down the shoreline highway, through fog thick as fingers and sudden bursts of rain that pound ferociously on the windshield for several minutes before retiring back into the clouds, low and grumbling. Graeme drives steadily and tells stories into a microphone, Scottish fables of kings and fairies and promiscuous women. Saucy Mary who bared her breasts to passing sailors as they entered island waters, collecting tariffs in the bib of her dress. And then one day Mary leaps into the sea, raging and screaming until finally she sinks, silent, still, weighted with gold.

As we turn inland and begin to slide between the mountain range, the blackface ewe makes her way to the crest of a jagged ridge. She has lost sight of her flock but is driven by instinct up and into the wind, as sheep often are. She has chewed her way along a path of wilted heather, the purple flowers whipping against her ankles as she staggers over loose stones and black mud and slips toward a white and opal sky.

Cynthia retires to her bed and Jon slowly gets up from a wooden attic floor. Vodka storms his bloodstream and, for the moment, he is calm. The lightbulb blinks inside the unfinished bathroom and he resolves to fix this first thing in the morning. Tomorrow his children will arrive—two teenagers now, a boy and a girl—and he will be sure to tell them this new plan: an electronics degree from Concordia Community College and an apartment across the street from their high school. He will tell them and tell them and tell them until he is sure that they understand. Then they will go for a spaghetti dinner in his mother's new car.

For now, Jon tucks his suitcase under the extra bed and folds down the blanket. He tightens the cap back onto an empty vodka bottle and stashes it in a dresser drawer. He looks through a window and watches the moon undress in the front yard. He remembers nights like this while camping in the Poconos with his brothers or sailing through the Chesapeake Bay, the moon naked over St. Michael's. *Fiery anchor. Steadfast woman.* He wants water and then sleep and so he heads to the stairs and fumbles for the railing in the semi-dark.

Here, at the crest of the mountain, the ewe can see a black swath of sea and beyond that, the ripened green swell of mainland. She has never left this island. Indeed, she has never left this particular mountainside. The neon-pink tag that dangles from her left ear marks her for this territory alone—which is every day new and terrifying and fixed just right in the vast stream of consciousness she has come to know. And this is just fine. And so it is also fine when the wind begins to taste thick and the heather on her tongue blows like hurricanes and the slim fissure between land and air dissolves and the sound of bleating sheep is just a cloud like any other. She whips her body right and left and, unblinking, lets the rain collect in the two black pockets of her eyes. When she falls she reaches her nose toward the soft gray space between this land and the next. She falls, and the taste of gray is acrid like dew on a familiar metal fence.

On the bus, I sit next to a curious man named Lin who wants to show me his very elaborate cell phone, which I cannot understand even after several demonstrations. He wants to know why I am on this bus with them—Why am I here? Where am I going?—and I try to tell him about the summer program at a British university and the rail pass that lets me wander the United Kingdom at will, and we try so hard to communicate that by the time the bus lurches to a stop I am no longer sure how I've gotten here myself. We stop in the middle of the road and I am almost certain that we have not made it to the island's unofficial capital, a seaside town called Portree. Graeme slams the bus into park and leaves us without a word, the open door shivering on rickety hinges as the wind continues to blow. We cannot see him through the windshield, opaque with fog. I hear him grunt once—"Shite"—as he stomps back onto the bus to gather a pair of muddy gloves from beneath the driver's seat. He faces us.

"Sheep," he says, and stomps down the steps and out to the road.

At the exact moment when, five years ago in April, Jon finally finds the railing, a single electrical charge wanders beyond its constituency. This tiny, hot-yellow pulse of energy sparks another and another and another, a lightning storm in the brain. Like a man in an electric chair, my father's body erupts in a series of violent convulsions, each muscle spurned out of complacency, and he falls, headfirst, down a single flight of stairs.

By the time Cynthia finds his body at ten o'clock the next morning it is cold, wide-eyed, a blue sea of skin in flannel, a single yellow boot. A healthier man would have survived that seizure, but my father's body couldn't take any more. It was waving the white flag, and in reply he said, "Fuck you," and took another shot. After he died we cleared our basement of his things, certain now that he would not return. Half-constructed model sailboats, boxes of old flyers for the construction business he had once failed to create, rusty tools and broken skis and fifty-seven empty bottles of vodka hidden in the crawl space. If he saw a light he would have steered toward it, elated to have finally found the way.

The carcass is a mound of snow. It is a pink, lunar heart. I watch from the side of the road as Graeme drags the ewe across the pavement, his glove and the cuff of his flannel shirt dipped in red like a candied apple. Her neck hangs limp over his forearm and a strip of black fur on her muzzle is peeled back to reveal the clean, pearlescent bone and the crimson underside of skin speckled with tiny stones. I cannot look away. I am stunned still by what seems to be an affirmation.

I never saw my father's body after he died. For a long time I was resentful that I hadn't been given the option. I don't remember asking to see him, but I do recall a day many weeks after the funeral, after the shock had worn off, when I realized I could have asked and hadn't. There wasn't a viewing. We didn't perform a wake. When I asked my mother about it she admitted she had gone to see his body in the hospital, but she'd felt she was protecting us by not bringing my brother and me along. I'd felt a sudden rush of anger and regret. There are reasons we sit with our dead. To bear witness is to usher them into death, and in kind, they return us to the land of the living. Because I seldom saw my father in the years prior, his final absence never felt real. It was like a fugue state, our twinned souls circling in purgatory. The ewe isn't my father, I know that, but this corpse, she is death itself. This is tangible. This I understand in a way that I need not translate to myself. There was nothing, nothing I could do.

I look and look and look. Graeme takes hold of the tag stapled through the ewe's ear and quickly tears it from the body, removing extra strips of skin and tucking it into his pocket.

"She's got to be claimed," he says, climbing onto the bus.

We settle back into the vinyl seats. Graeme puts the bus in gear and we continue down the empty road. He is a young man, his face pocked with scars. He is solid with strong, blunt hands. He is building a hostel of his own during the winter months when he isn't giving tours, a log cabin on the Isle of Mull where he grew up. Graeme clears his throat and drives fast. He speaks into the microphone and watches us in the rearview mirror.

"Sometimes," he says, "sometimes the heather is dead and dry and the sheep eat it and get stoned—hallucinate, like magic mushrooms. Some seasons we have to be very careful. They fall from the sky and land on the roofs of the cars. They think they can fly. That ewe thought she could fly."

I've heard about this phenomenon before, of some animals imbibing just as recklessly as humans: deer tipsy on late-season apples and goats that climb to the tallest peaks of the Rockies to chew on high-altitude weeds that get them, well, high. And like their human counterparts, animals are most vulnerable to the lure of altered reality when times get tough, right before hibernation or during the deep cold of mid-winter.

He fingers the plastic tag in his pocket and thinks about the man he'll later call to report the accident. A jovial farmer named Pete who has lost more sheep than any other man on the island, which Graeme feels is a shame and yet, a little funny, too.

Once, when Eric and I were young, Jon was in a bad car accident. Our mother roused us in the middle of the night and shuffled us, lank and ghostlike, into the backseat of the old blue car. We drove the empty streets in silence, save for our mother's muffled swears and my brother's bare feet kicking at the back of the front seat. We'd done this before. If he could avoid the police, if the accident was just between him and the inanimate objects littering his way, Jon would call us to come get him before the neighbors got nosy. I never knew what became of the crumpled cars and trucks. As far as I knew they were left right there, like dejected toys.

We found his battered truck in a ShopRite parking lot, the smashed headlights still pulsing lazily into the mist like two dying fireflies. The parking lot was empty except for the truck, a few wayward shopping carts, and the streetlight that had blocked my father's passage. I wasn't yet able to distinguish my waking life from my dream life, and so it all felt like fantastic fun. I knew money didn't grow on trees, but it did spew from machines just by someone tapping a few buttons. Likewise, bodies were a given and death was an illusion. Nighttime was the stuff of movies and dreams and so was without consequence. Whatever unfolded in the cover of dark was a separate reel. Its only link to the calm of morning coffee and cartoons were the thin threads of memory, and I knew that couldn't be trusted.

When he got into the car he was wet with blood and something else, something glittery spread into the new yellow hairs along his chin. When he turned around to face us I could see a swathe of shattered glass smeared over his skin like tiny kernels of sand. I thought he was beautiful, a beautiful shimmery monster in the flashing light of another broken car. My mother looked straight ahead and said nothing.

"I got you guys something," he said. "Candy."

My mother whipped her head around.

"No!" she said. "Don't you give them anything."

I felt my brother reach out in the dark as my mother smacked away my father's hand, the two pink sugar cubes clattering onto the metal floor.

"Your fucking hands are covered in blood!"

"It's only candy, for God's sake! It's wrapped."

But he didn't say any more, just sat there mute as we drove home, his magic cheek turning colors with the changing stoplights on the way.

Slowly, I reached down and collected our treats from the floor. I unwrapped them quietly and shoved them both into my mouth. I let the pink sugar melt slowly and silently onto my tongue and finally I fell asleep on my brother's lap, content.

Until a few months earlier, Jon had been sober for a year. He'd taken us to the Poconos to teach us to ski. When we arrived, he dressed us in six layers of clothing each and sent us out to get a feel for our new mobility. After he finally left the lodge, he found us both at the top of the mountain. Somehow, we had managed to figure out the ski lift on our own. I heard my father calling to us from the lift, "Don't move!" We were unaccustomed to such forceful, masculine instruction. We froze, clutching at each other's arms until Eric began to giggle helplessly beneath his two woolen caps and I couldn't hold back; I began to laugh, too. I remember how red our father's face became as he realized that we no longer took him seriously. By the time he reached us he was not angry, but stiff with embarrassment.

We took off down the mountainside, our little bodies banging into one another, barely upright, barely controlled. Our father passed us, demonstrating the "pizza slice," a way of narrowing the skis into a point in front of you to manage your speed. We picked this up immediately and began to move more slowly, delighting in the mastery over our own skinny limbs. I held Eric's hand. We were too small yet for poles. As our father sped ahead, we lost sight of him in a great flourish of snow, but we were confident he would find us at the bottom, scoop us up, and take us onto the lift for another try. And then, incredibly, he did.

THE
DOLLHOUSE

MY FATHER WAS Cynthia's firstborn and she likes to tell the story of his beginning. I am twelve and sit cross-legged on an Oriental rug inside the townhouse she bought after divorcing my grandfather. She rocks in her rocking chair and works a needle through the hem of my overlong pants. I sit rapt, a blanket over my bare legs, popping cold green grapes into my mouth and chewing like a cow.

"Don't chew like a cow, child," she scolds. "You'll get fat like Helen."

Helen is my mother's mother and my love for her is uncomplicated and soothing, like cake. It is different with Cynthia, I am realizing, though I haven't seen much of her since I was eight and she and my grandfather moved to South Carolina after his retirement. Now she is back in Pennsylvania and I am learning how to please her. I wear the shiny penny loafers she bought for me at Lord & Taylor and call my brother *icky* because all males, according to Cynthia, are *icky*. She does not invite Eric over. It is the beginning of a swift and merciless erasure, my brother's gender relegating him to nonpersonhood. She does not call or speak to him and nobody understands why. Cynthia had four sons and has buried one already, though two more are slouching ever closer and there is nothing she can do about it. Eric, it seems, might as well join them now and without much fuss. "I'm no good for boys," is all she will say when pressed, though I rarely press. Her wrath is unpredictable and I know, even at twelve, that my abdication would be forever. She refers to me as her daughter and speaks of my mother (once her pet, too, and now, it seems, her competition) as if she is no better than the squirrels digging in her trash cans.

"Well, I was the one who had to pay for all those abortions," she says to me casually one day. "Oh, you didn't know? A ploy to keep your father around, that's for sure."

But here on her rug, one winter day when I am twelve, crackling heat rushing from the fireplace, the soles of my feet warm and the bursting grapes sweet and pulpy as I chew one and then another, I feel only gratitude for my inexplicable specialness, my new role as the chosen one. I do not yet realize how many have come before me, that each of her sons received this same treatment at one time or another—the shopping sprees and chin-lifting adulations—and that my own mother, whom she now so disdains, was once her "daughter," too, a thin girl from a middle-class Jewish family who ogled what seemed only opulence and discretion, the new boyfriend's family like a wealthier version of the Cleavers, practically aristocratic, the very blood in their veins like gilded silk.

Cynthia was an only child from a small town in Illinois and she loved her father with singular ferocity. He sold high-end lawn mowers for a company named Barbara-Greene. He also flew small single-engine planes over wheat-cracked fields and once, in the 1920s, before he married my great-grandmother, he fell in love with a Parisian burlesque dancer named Lucienne. Her photograph hung behind Cynthia's desk for years: Lucienne's small perfect breasts bare between the sparkly straps that hold up a large billowy skirt. She wears ballet slippers, her ankles crossed in perfect fifth position, and her plump white arms reach high over her head, her fingers laced into the plume of peacock feathers she wears on her back. Her expression is girlish and amused. If sadness is there, I don't see it. She smiles with one side of her mouth. Her eyes are dark and round and lined in kohl beneath straight black bangs.

Cynthia had many fantasies about Lucienne's life, as she did about any lifestyle she imagined exotic, and she whispered them to me gleefully when I was a child, as if relating the red pockets of her own past. She lamented how her father's parents had forced him back to Illinois to marry a local girl who cooked well and collected porcelain. She imagined his alternate life the way most girls covet fairy tales; she spoke of dark curtains and snifters of brandy and crinoline petticoats hiked above Lucienne's knees, her thighs cold and chiseled like marble. But there was propriety in it, too, because Cynthia was a woman who valued intellect and social status above all else, and she learned to play puppeteer to her loved ones with long strings of money. And so Lucienne is an orphan escaped from a rural convent and forced into the sordid life of the Folies Bergère, until one day she meets my great-grandfather and is given the opportunity of education, Cambridge or Oxford of course, where she becomes a brilliant art historian, traveling the world on cruise ships with her devoted husband, her early career just a cheeky anecdote revealed to certain enlightened company during small but decadent dinner parties.

I found these stories mesmerizing, even while I recognized the essential misconceptions that made them possible. They were fascinating because they revealed a softer side to my grandmother, a glimpse of the woman beneath the facade of doctor's wife, church choir soprano, and country club denizen. As I got older, I learned to distinguish the many layers of Cynthia—many personalities even—each with its own voice and posture and set of values. But they took years to learn, years in which Cynthia shed her family and friends like dead skin, a gradual sloughing of excess souls, until it became just her and me on the telephone, a young woman she exalted and lavished with money and attention, a relationship as fantastic as any fable and just as dangerous. *I am your fairy godmother*, she often sang out in the middle of conversation, her voice a mercurial liquid silver.

Now that Cynthia is dead, Lucienne is above my desk. I talk to her. She is my confidant, my silent partner, an empty vessel into which I pour my stories. She does not breathe a word. She is sexless, heartless; her skin is bleached. She is a doll that I can arrange at whim, as I once was, ragged and mean. I wish I could dig my knuckles into her spine and pull those tender shoulders back against my chest.

Hold your shoulders back, child. You have such lousy posture.

My Lucienne is smart but ineffectual and greedy in the hungry way of the young. I send her abroad and buy her pretty dresses and expensive scarves. I pay her way to Italy, England, Scotland, and Ireland. She studies art, history, and the literature of decadence: Oscar Wilde and Vernon Lee and Robert Browning. She is my world, my pigeon, *my little pet*. Perhaps she is half-*Jewish*, my Lucienne, my beautiful belle. She is not to tell and not to use *those* words, her mother's words—*oy* and *kepala* and *kvetch*—they only make her sound dumb. Even now, I must help her tidy her sloppy sexuality, her stringy clothing, her countless mispronunciations. A silly girl who needs fixing.

My mother was fourteen when Cynthia swept her into the fold. The four Nelson boys each drove expensive but practical cars. They snuck out at night, drank themselves sick, and in the morning came down to breakfast donning neckties. They attended (and were summarily expelled from) various boarding schools in New England. When Cynthia came upon a glass bong in the basement one day, she mistook it for a vase and filled it with fresh water and a handful of white lilies from the garden.

There were prime ribs for supper and fences to keep the deer from dining on prize-winning rhododendrons. A gardener named José and a beautiful Jamaican housekeeper named Icy. A grand piano. Cynthia was learning the violin. My grandfather,

Harry, nipped at bottles of gin squirreled away in the cushions of his easy chair and tugged on a pipe, bergamot-laced smoke tumbling over the fat drowsing cat they called Floosy.

It was an intoxicating narrative, you understand. My mother's father sold upholstery; her mother, real estate. They did not vacation in Bermuda, but down the Jersey Shore. Year after year after year. And when Cynthia stole my mother's favorite synthetic-blend sweater and sliced it to pieces with her sewing shears, they all had a good laugh. There would be better sweaters soon. Countless cashmere sweaters and matching pearls.

But enough. I am twelve and I want news of my father. I rarely see him anymore and so she tells me this story.

It was 1958 and Jon was still churning inside her belly while the blows of Chicago's most violent snowstorm were still at bay. She did not yet realize all the damage it would do, that she would be right there, in the eye of the storm. She was a new wife and living in Philadelphia with my grandfather Harry, who attended medical school at the University of Pennsylvania. She did not love this man, not really, but had married him to please her mother—a stony woman who'd been drawn to the scent of old money wafting from the Nelson family home, from gleaming mahogany chests and the warm flanks of the thoroughbred horses as they stood stomping and snuffing inside the stables. The cinnamon smell of the maid's slick, black, and shining skin. A doctor's wife, her mother had cried out after receiving news of the engagement. Her heart was an empty bank vault, Cynthia tells me, and I believe her, believe most anything she tells me for a very long time.

Jon craved red meat and so she ate it, rare at first, thick steaks singed and peppered black on the surface, wet and crimson inside. It would not do; it was raw flesh he demanded—needed, she supposed—some prenatal nutrient gone missing from the modern diet, and so she pried apart small strips of the uncooked steaks and sucked them down greedily, stealthily, until Harry caught her one day and snapped, "Cynthia!" She'd felt ashamed and stupid and didn't eat much of anything after that.

"That was my first mistake," she says.

She gestures me close and helps me into my newly hemmed pants. She does not hug me or pinch my *tuchus* like Helen, but she pats my head and blinks, her eyes giant blue marbles like Louise's, my favorite doll's. Louise has three yarns of yellow hair that I twirl around my tongue until they yield like chewing gum. In this way I fall asleep most every night. Cynthia gave me Louise when I was just a baby and she will periodically confiscate her and give her a good scrubbing. Cynthia's hair is soft as rabbit fur and she lets me fluff it sometimes when she is using her baby girl voice, which she uses now, and there is much blinking and mewing and oh, she loves me so.

"I flew to Illinois. I was eight months pregnant. Daddy was away on a business trip and had begged me to come home and look after Mother while he was gone. I agreed, out of boredom, I suppose, and devotion to Daddy. It was a Saturday when I arrived," she says. "I know it was a Saturday because the milk was out, in the bottles, you know?"

But of course I don't know, being twelve and morose and narrow-sighted.

"When Mother answered the door she just stared at me. She was wearing this white silk robe I couldn't recall. She must have thought me fat, fat, fat. And I was. 'Well, come in child,' she said. 'You're letting all the good air out.' Can you imagine, Jessie? Oh, it was an ugly house! Cheap, cheap!"

She lifts her arms in front of her and lets her wrists dangle as she flutters her fingers about. It is a silent request for me to hold her hands, which I grant her eagerly, because physical affection from Cynthia is rare—or at least it is never enough for me, so accustomed to the hugging and kissing and cuddling from my mother's side of the family.

I WILL RECALL this conversation years later, as an adult, when I arrive at her deathbed and startle her out of a morphine coma.

"Gramma, it's me, Jessie!" I cry out. "I'm here."

I won't mean to cry, but the suddenness of her condition will undo knots and scrape the sky out.

An email from Harry's third wife on another Saturday morning:

"We have sad news. Grandma/Cynthia is in critical condition after having been diagnosed last Wednesday with pancreatic cancer and metastases to her liver. She is not responding but is getting excellent care at the nursing wing at Foulkeways where she has been living."

Beyond the inappropriateness of an email in such a situation, it is the duplicitous mention of her, "Grandma/Cynthia," that will dissolve any last notions that this is a family. When

I finally get to her from Connecticut, two hours later, she is already beyond language, and there is only this final expression of her.

"It's me, Gramma. Jessie. Can you open your eyes?"

When she does, I will see that I've scared her terribly, suddenly wrested her from whatever hollow of peace the drugs had carved out, her blue eyes shot through with electric yellow, the liver quickly expiring (weary, punched out), and her arms will lift and her fingers will flutter and her expression will send screws tumbling to the floor—an image that will beat itself out inside me for weeks and months and maybe forever—her mouth contorted in the most awful grimace of hopelessness and anger and utter disappointment. Even though I am assured by the nurses that this has nothing to do with consciousness, with agency, with message, but only with the helpless contractions of a body shutting down, I cannot help but feel that I have let her down, again and now eternally, and I will never know why. More than likely, this is the ego at work, a terrible self-importance compelling me to believe her ultimate act of will would be for me, albeit one of scorn, and that she would use any last shreds of selfhood in order to get this message across. But because I can't know, because she did not phone me the week before, when she first learned of her terminal diagnosis, nor in the days that followed, I cannot help but wonder and despair at the thought of her loneliness, her fear, and what may have kept her from reaching out to me then, as she did with most any other grievance. Was it merely to protect me? Or was it because she had decided that her final days would be her own, away from the tears and terror of people who had already mourned so many, and so loudly? Certainly, a little quiet might be in order. I ought to honor her bravery—that she would climb so quietly into her deathbed and politely offer up her arm for the morphine drip that, she must have known, would take away her volition for good. While I had often felt that she was living her life through me, offering up the pleasures of travel and education, she had never suggested that I had any right to her death, too. I had assumed that this singular love meant that she would want me near her in those closing days, the only person she seemed to trust, and that she would have some last wisdom to impart, some direction to offer to a life in which she had seemed so vested, and yet so quickly abandoned. In turn, I thought I could offer all of me, just this once, which is what she had always wanted after all.

I was wrong. I should have stayed away. She had a right to her privacy, and selfishly, I took it from her when she needed it most.

After her funeral, a woman named Gerry will introduce herself as Cynthia's driver.

"What a relief it must have been for her," she will say to me. "Why, just last week she told me how she was never loved."

I tried to love her, had wished to love her, at least. I wanted to explain how draining she could be, how she called obsessively, how she pretended we hadn't spoken for months when we'd been on the phone for hours only the day before. That the conversation was always the same. ("No, I haven't spoken to Grandpa. No, I can't be a tenured professor right now.")

I'll want to defend myself from charges no one is making but me—that my grandmother frustrated me, that I often avoided her calls or made excuses to get off the phone, that I still let her pay my exorbitant rent while I was in graduate school and accepted the trips she funded. That I sometimes let her put down my mother and brother because I was afraid she would stop paying my rent if I argued. That I believe this makes me a bad person and so I try to avoid thinking about it.

"Will you remember me?" she had often asked in the months before her death, before I had any clue that it was so imminent. "Will you write about me?" She had been planning her death all along, and I just didn't see it.

After she dies, I take a budding Christmas cactus from her room and place it on my windowsill where, every day, it strains to drink up the few hours of winter sun. And every morning for weeks I will find another pink bud abandoned on the Formica, like the pretty heads of decapitated queens, snapped off for want of light.

"We mostly spoke about bridge club," she tells me as I hop around in my new pants, "my mother's weekly rendezvous with her lady friends. They were to arrive the next morning for a game."

Cynthia had dinner with her mother: great gobs of mashed potatoes and wet fish in melted butter.

"I remember her drinking a martini and thinking how it must sting to lick booze over her cracked lips. Sip, lick, sip, lick. Like so. But that's the sort of woman she was, you see; she'd get some satisfaction out of that, I suppose. Oh, but

Jessie, it was a great big howling monster of a storm. *Woooo, woooo,*" she said, imitating the wind.

After dinner, Cynthia had sat in a chair with a blanket over her ankles.

"How is that doctor of yours?" her mother had called out from the kitchen.

I imagine my great-grandmother's fingers tense around a silver shaker. I use some vague version of Maggie Smith from *A Room With a View,* since I've never actually seen a photo of my great-grandmother. I give her blue eyes like Cynthia's and dark upswept hair. I hear the spoon clanking in the sink and then a long silence.

I lick grape juice over my lips and feel a burn, a satisfaction, and then a familiar shame.

"Harry is fine, of course," Cynthia had replied.

"Though I was really picturing him gone, run off, dead," she confides to me now. She giggles and I giggle back. She likes me best when we are in cahoots.

She had watched the snowdrifts in the light of streetlamps, tossed skyward like the risen dead. My father, unborn and belly warm, pedaled softly against her ribs. The grandfather clock chimed the hours and she fell asleep, a newspaper over her stomach like a paper tent.

She woke to the smack of ice and sleet against the side of the house. She tried to turn on a lamp but the power had gone out.

"I thought I heard snoring but no, Mother was not asleep at all. I heard this gurgling or weeping. I couldn't quite make it out."

Cynthia hoisted herself up and went looking for a flashlight, finding one tucked away beneath a cabinet full of porcelain figurines, each a gift from Cynthia's paternal grandmother. "Another woman of taste, my mother always said." She fingered a glittering young peasant boy, a brown pail tucked beneath his shoulder. His blue eyes were delicately painted to look as if he were peering to the right. As her mother sobbed or gurgled or whatever it was that Cynthia suspected she may have been doing, Cynthia slipped him into her pocket before padding down the hallway, lightly pushing on her mother's bedroom door. She was not in bed. She heard her soft whimpering, a heaving sound, and then silence. Tiptoeing toward the window, my grandmother shone her flashlight over her mother's frail body, twisted on the floor and caught between the bed and the wall, her nightgown soaked with vomit. She was very drunk.

"I said, 'Get up! Get up!' but her eyes were rolled back into her head and I thought her dead. It was a great relief, Jessie, you must understand. She was very evil." She draws out the word "evil" like a cartoon character. "She was not like you at all, dear. You are good! My pet, my little pigeon!"

My great-grandmother had whimpered again and flailed, wrenching forward, another stream of vomit pouring onto her lap. Grasping her beneath the armpits, Cynthia pulled her up and rolled her onto the bed.

"Looking at her lying there, crooked and pale, I was so afraid. Not for her, or for myself, but for your daddy, inside me, oblivious. I sometimes think he felt my fear, that this doomed him somehow. Still, I feel very ashamed."

This was the first and last time I ever heard Cynthia speak explicitly of guilt, of maternal guilt in particular, the very crux of her that becomes like a black cancer, small and hard and hidden beneath stoic resignation. *Oh, these things happen,* she will say when my father dies. *This is just what happens.* And then one day, when Eric was seventeen and I was nineteen, my mother finally called up the courage to confront Cynthia over the phone about her indifference toward Eric. During my next visit, a few days later, I found several photos of him as a child strewn about her dining room table, as if she had been trying desperately to dredge up some long-forgotten feeling for him. I suppose she didn't find it, there in his gap-toothed smile, because she never brought it up.

Cynthia had loved her four sons. Her love, when she showed it, was full-press and unflinching. She found their teenage antics amusing and giggled conspiratorially when she learned that they had been leaping from the second-floor windows in the dead of night. She thought their gumption was hysterical, their very boy-ness a strange anthropological discovery. They would beat each other bloody on the lawn and Cynthia could only shriek and patter away. *Eek!* she would cry, covering her eyes.

When my mother first inquired about her seizure disorder, which was lifelong and controlled by medication, Cynthia explained that it was usually brought on by flashing lights, at which point my father began rapidly flicking the light switch.

"Aah! See? They want me dead!" she called out, laughing.

There was a playfulness to her relationships with her sons, a sense of humor that they could not share with Harry, the stoic patriarch. Once, they rented a house on Hilton Head Island that backed up to a public beach and had its own swimming pool. My father and Harry were off somewhere and so my mother, Eric, Cynthia, and I decided to make use of the pool. I remember my shock when Cynthia suddenly dropped her towel and dove into the water naked.

"Be free!" she had squealed, her white round breasts smacking the surface of the water like flapjacks.

It was this Cynthia I liked the best, the emboldened pixie, the overgrown child. My mother and brother also went naked and when it was my turn to ditch my swimming suit, I did so with great reticence and cried for hours after Eric tossed it far onto the beach, so that to retrieve it I had to run bare-assed over the hot sand. My mother and Cynthia found my modesty hilarious. After all, I was eight and flat-chested, a mere child, and therefore without possession of a Body with a capital B. What was there to be embarrassed about?

Like an older sister, my mother often exploited my insecurities for her own amusement. Later that same week, she suddenly pulled down my pants on a crowded dock and I froze, my underpants around my ankles, until she stopped laughing long enough to come help me pull them up again. I was so stunned I couldn't move. My mother's jokes were never meant to be cruel; she just couldn't understand how any child of hers could take herself so seriously.

"Get a grip!" she likes to say.

As I get older and my self-consciousness gets sanded down to a duller shade of red, I can appreciate her antics.

"Oh, you're a little funny," she will say occasionally, surprised at some joke I've pulled at my own expense. "I'd thought only Eric and I were funny."

It is this part of their relationship that I can never fully enter. I am too square or too solemn or too judgmental. And it was this part of Cynthia's relationship with her sons that Harry never understood. I cannot presume to know the exact nature of their undoing, but when Cynthia insisted my mother drive eight hours down to South Carolina to fetch her after suddenly leaving Harry after fifty-eight years of marriage—despite my mother's own failing marriage, despite my father's latest debilitating binge, no matter the two small children my mother had to care for ("You must get me now!" Cynthia had demanded. "Enough about you!")—she came back with a fever hotter than hell and a new self-sufficiency that was cutting and cruel. Embracing her new independence seemed to demand total extrication from anyone who might need or give love. That part of her life was over, at least for a long time. She bought herself a townhouse and furnished it with opulent Oriental rugs and a grand piano. She had china shipped in from England and a hard, white, damask sofa. She made Eric and me a guest room on the third floor, though I think he was invited to stay only once. It was in that same guest room, six years later, where my father would spend his last weeks and where Cynthia would find him, one cool morning in April, crumpled, blue, and dead at the bottom of the stairs.

AFTER SHE'D FOUND her mother on the floor, Cynthia called the paramedics, but they were slow to arrive because of all the snow. Her mother toyed with them. They couldn't take her away without her consent.

"Hello, boys," she had whispered as they came in.

One man grabbed her wrist for a pulse. Another gathered the cord of an IV.

"You came to see something, eh, boys? Is that right?" she said slyly, parting her legs, her nightgown wide like an open mouth. "Listen, boys," she said, "I'm not going anywhere, so you can take your hands off of me unless you'd like to do something useful with them."

They let her go.

"Can you be a little tough, boys? Are you men or are you boys? What's it going to be?"

From the other side of the room, Cynthia had to watch them gather their things and put their instruments away, mumbling softly as they walked toward the door.

My father was the second of Cynthia's sons to die. David followed a few years later, swallowing a handful of Klonopin before walking into a hospital cafeteria, ordering a tuna fish sandwich, and collapsing dead on the floor. The first Eric, my brother's namesake, died in a car accident when he was fifteen. He'd been driving around with some friends and drinking cans of Labatt Blue before visiting my father at the convenience store where he was working.

I imagine they bought cigarettes. I imagine they talked about the night ahead, about girls, perhaps, and an upcoming party.

Or they stood around in the parking lot for a while, smoking the cigarettes and nudging each other off the curb, spitting onto the pavement and watching their shoes, hands in pockets, their long hair tucked beneath wool caps. It was March, so there must have been gray clouds of breath rising into a black sky. They may have seen stars and a moon, or else there was a curtain of frozen air pulled tight like a shroud.

My father said goodbye to his brother and Eric nodded, tossed his cigarette, and climbed into the back seat of his friend's car.

My father went inside, the bell ringing on the door, and the boys drove a mile down the street, lost control, and catapulted into a tree. The driver lived but the other three boys died instantly.

Was that it then? The loss that had broken my grandmother's already fragile composure?

Had she settled into her life? Had she put away her fantasies and found some comfort in the routines of motherhood just before it all came undone? I'd always wanted to ask her, but never dared. She seldom spoke about Eric, by all accounts a handsome and funny boy whom his brothers, my father especially, admired and toddled after, basking in the glow of his charisma. But isn't that always the case, after they're gone?

"Do you know my brother Eric?" my father asked my mother soon after they met. "You'll love him. All the girls do."

I often wondered if he'd meant that as a boast or a word of caution. *You may like me now, but not after you meet Eric.* I found that story surprising because I'd always imagined my father as the most handsome and popular of boys. That was the story I'd been told. But later a different version surfaced and it made more sense. My father was a smart and quiet man who built model sailboats in the basement and constructed rudimentary computers from spare parts (from nothing more, it seemed to me, than fishing wire and an old icebox). He could make anything work, except of course, his own splintered psyche. So, it was this side of him I could imagine as the follower: the thoughtful boy drinking too much in the corner to cover up his shyness, daydreaming about sailboats and trout fishing, or camping alone high in the Tetons.

Half-baked business schemes were a necessity after children came along, not (as I'd once thought) the stuff of dreams. My father devised and demolished nearly a dozen businesses in half as many years before even that much effort became absurd. As kids, Eric and I would spend days on end in his office stuffing envelopes with flyers for Nelson Brothers' Construction, or Nelson Computers, or Nelson Asbestos Removal, none of which lasted more than a few months. After he died, I often felt like my brother and I were just more unfinished business. When he failed, our father would retreat to the basement with a bottle of vodka and some hobby glue, tenderly affixing miniature sails to the mast of another doomed ship.

"I think now if only they had been an hour earlier, if only they had gotten to her before she woke up," Cynthia said.

But what, I wondered, *did she imagine would have been avoided?*

She is a new character now. Not the little girl but the shrewd sophisticate, a role I always imagined Judi Dench might play in the movie of her life. She straightens and looks down at me, a raven preparing for flight. I am out of grapes and the fire has burned down to ash.

"When they left she hissed at me and called me a little bitch. My own mother said that to me." Cynthia starts to rise.

She is grinding her teeth and stretching her neck, one eye moving about in its socket, roaming and reptilian. She opens her mouth as if to crow, as if to call out the day. I do not like this story anymore. I am scared and I listen for my mother's car horn to rescue me, but it doesn't come, not yet.

"I heard voices, Jessie. I heard voices and saw visions: my son screaming out and my father chuckling softly into his newspaper and Harry grunting and moaning. Oh, that moaning! I saw my mother as she was when I was a child, sweeping and dancing and drinking and clawing at the door when Daddy locked her up to dry her out."

She is stamping her foot and the loose skin underneath her chin shivers like pond water and I picture my daddy as a little boy, waving goodbye as Harry drives her away to the psych ward where she spent eight months being put back together like a rickety doll come undone.

"Mothers are no good, Jessie. Mothers are no good."

She is loudly alone. I see the cracks for the first time, and the tenuous threads of the hack jobs that keep us together. I feel for my own seams and wonder, dumbly, when they, too, will start to tear.

"When you're ready to divorce 'em," Cynthia confided to my mother one day, "you do it so fast it makes their head spin."

In other words, get out before they have the chance to lawyer up. Always the more financially savvy of the two, Cynthia made out just fine after the divorce. While Harry had earned the money, Cynthia knew how to invest it. Newly single and financially independent, she decided she would go into voice acting and hired a coach to help her develop a demo tape. She had her picture taken by a professional photographer and sent the photos along with the tapes. She never got a gig, but as a kid I marveled at this new tenacity, this belated drive to remake herself into something other than housewife and mother. If there she had failed, perhaps this is where she could flourish. And she was good, too. After she died, I found boxes of unsent demo tapes tucked into a closet in her apartment, detritus of the career that never was. I listened to the tapes obsessively on the flight back home to New York after her funeral, her voice swinging effortlessly from the smooth seduction of a yogurt aficionado into the brusque staccato of the drug rep hawking her wares. Here, all of her personalities were on display: the mischievous child, the no-bullshit intellectual, the doting mother, the flighty old bat hankering for a bowl of Breyers ice cream. She could be all of them at once and I was sorry she hadn't been given a chance.

"Stop it," I say. "Please stop this now," I say.

"Mothers are no good. Mothers are no good," Cynthia repeats.

Her expression terrifies me, as if she has gone somewhere else and left me alone. I am so quiet I barely hear myself. It is more exhalation than protest, and Cynthia seems not to notice, though she sits back down and begins rocking again, only vaguely aware, it seems, of the girl gone slack at her feet.

"Oh, but I woke to the sun!" She smiles and lays her head back against the chair. "There is something wholly rectifying about a Midwestern sun, even in winter. Mother was laughing, laughing, and someone said, 'Oh, Judy!' and it occurred to me then, as I lay in bed, that she had been up for hours. Her hair done, her makeup carefully lined and brushed and blotted. There was lemonade in a pitcher and fresh fruit in a dish. Two decks of red and blue cards were certainly on the dining room table, shuffled many times. And she had already worried over that lovely porcelain boy, absent from his spot on the shelf."

I AM BEQUEATHED an oversized diamond ring, a stuffed bear dressed in infant's cotton pajamas, and a box of new and used toiletries, including forty-four individually wrapped bars of Dove soap. All of her surviving grandchildren were with her in her final days, though she wasn't aware of it and wouldn't have wanted to be. What she had wanted, I am sure, was to be left alone.

A bedside radio played opera. She breathed mechanically, as if intubated, but she was not. When the last visitors left, I sat and held her hand and watched her body slowly die. Nurses came and went, changing her diaper and moving the window shades up and down and coating her face in sweet-smelling lotion. I read stories aloud and tried to think of things to say, but there was nothing really after all, except *I love you I love you*

I love you. I wore one of the turtleneck sweaters she'd bought for me and a pair of wool slacks. *A brownnoser outfit,* my mother would call it, and it was. I was frightened by how quickly her skin turned yellow and I dabbed furiously at the white foam that bubbled over her bottom lip and down her chin.

"What is that?" I demanded of the nurses, and they answered patiently and gave me a pile of clean rags with which to wipe her down.

Her tongue hung thick over her white teeth like a hooked fish. She breathed one-two, one-two. I filed her nails.

Then the nurse pressed her neck with two fingers and nodded and brushed back her curly hair.

That night I dreamed of cool black well water, of mothers like cake, of splitting seeds and the divested bone, of living boys with tender mouths and kisses on the cheek, of perfect Parisian dolls in perfect time, of silence and willful creatures, of flying full-faced toward a Midwestern sun.

She comes to her funeral in a tiny box and her accountant, Emory, a kind man resembling Abraham Lincoln, tells funny stories by her grave. It is next to my father's grave and Uncle Eric's, which is more weathered. Uncle David is buried next to his infant daughter two towns over. My brother Eric, newly sober and handsome beneath a sable sky, holds my hand tightly. The beautiful Jamaican housekeeper, Icy, shows up after having been unceremoniously fired twenty years before. She weeps openly and with her whole body. I think that such a physical display of emotion would have unnerved Cynthia, that she would have tittered, or maybe that isn't right at all.

"That woman saved my life," Icy sobs again and again.

We believe that Cynthia may have helped her gain citizenship and possibly bought her a modest home. She clutches at Eric and me and calls us her babies. Eric walks her to her car and holds the door as she climbs inside.

"You're a good boy," she says and smiles. "A very good boy," which is exactly what he does not hear enough.

Before we leave, I see Eric walk up to Emory. Both men bow their heads and look at their shiny black shoes. My brother lights a cigarette and puts one hand in his jacket pocket.

"I was just wondering," he says, "did my grandmother ever mention me?"

Emory unbuttons his jacket and exhales through his nose. He puts his hand on Eric's shoulder and pulls him close, squinting into the wind.

During the summer of 2009, two years before she died, Cynthia took me on a cruise around the British Isles. It was an extravagant trip and I was both grateful and not, reticent to spend two weeks alone with her but thrilled to see more of the world. She treated me like a princess, taking me on shopping sprees through Harrods and Jenners, hordes of salesgirls fawning over me as if I were famous. We bought Gucci purses and Christian Louboutin shoes, a trousseau of lingerie and bottles of perfume that glittered like finely cut crystal. It was so far out of my realm of experience that I had a hard time taking it all in. In my real life, I struggled to buy cereal. She spent twice my student debt on luxury items. I couldn't understand it. Had I asked her to instead pay off my loans she would have been galled, though she'd always preached education above all else. Her generosity was on her terms and was meant to buy my affection, and I had let it.

My favorite memory of Cynthia is something she made up. While she was often silly and helpless on this trip, donning her sunglasses while allowing the crew to wheel her around the ship (though she could walk when she wanted), she recounted a story afterward that never happened.

"You were so wonderful to me when I fell off the bed," she said over the phone one day, months after our return. "Do you remember? The ship was tossing around and I fell between the bed and the wall. You walked in and I called out to you, 'Jessie? Jessie? I'm over here!' And you pulled me right up onto that bed."

She laughed. I laughed back. I didn't have the heart to say it never happened. She wanted to believe I would save her if I could.

HEIGHT
OF THE
LAND

NICK AND I leave at night, in the cold, with a thermos of over-steeped tea dripping onto the porch. We leave in our woolen hats, me in my mittens and downy winter coat, he in his flannel shirt and the tattered blue jeans that fall just a bit too short, ankles exposed. He calls his flannel a "jacket" because he grew up in Maine where "blood runs thick" and "sweat is saltier and does not freeze." We walk cautiously and hold hands, feeling in the dark for cracks in the wooden porch and the heavy, cumbrous ice slicks that settle over the steps. We are leaving like "thieves in the night," he says, vulpine and furtive, through a cloud of hot breath and steamy chamomile.

We just had sex on the living room floor, and for once I didn't cry as I came, didn't glimpse that small death just over the precipice.

I am going away again—I am excited—and he is going back, but we are *going*, and this is what matters. I like going, leaving, moving. Only yesterday I returned from a study abroad program in Italy, returned to the empty apartment and the abandoned college town of Durham. The roommates were still at their parents' places, in slippers, feasting on Thanksgiving leftovers, turkey sandwiches and twice-baked potatoes. Nick picked me up at the airport in Manchester, New Hampshire, and we drove the hour back to Durham in near silence. We were groggy and disoriented from the sudden evaporation of distance, of the two months spent apart, unlearning the body. But it was not an uncomfortable silence, and I watched cows mill around the mud-slicked barns outside the window and he occasionally played with my hair. I stuck my finger in his ear and twice shoved a hand down his pants.

At the bottom of the steps, I hear the shuffling of the caged raccoon. He is tucked beneath the porch and looks out at us with raging yellow eyes, like neon blinkers reaching out from the depths of a black hole. His warm body heaves steadily inside the metal cage. A shackled creature, those terrible eyes like portals to some ghostly landscape where we might all quietly go mad, where I could placidly shed my clothes and roll in shit and chew on the cheeks of rodents.

The trap was rigged up this morning by Animal Services and baited with chicken bones. The raccoon had been spotted several times in daylight and the neighbors feared rabies. Six traps were set up around my block, under eaves and in the dusty forgotten corners of garages. Somehow, I knew he would end up with me, rattling all day from beneath my porch. I listened from the kitchen window, afraid to go outside.

"I'm putting him in the car," Nick says. "We'll drop him off somewhere far away."

He tugs his gloves on tighter, like a man in a boxing ring. He has the look of a welterweight, compact and quick, though he wears a lot of flannel shirts and jeans that are always a touch too short. Still, this is a handsome man: chiseled jaw and movie-star blue eyes, his thick sandy-colored hair cut short lest it begin to resemble a helmet. When he bends to pick up the cage, his shirt slides up his back and I glimpse skin so pale it glows. He looks excited, skittish, like he has an urge to wrestle the wild forces of nature. This look makes me nervous, for the raccoon and for myself.

"The hell you are," I say. "Animal Services is coming to get him in the morning. They'll do the dropping." The raccoon begins to scramble inside his cage. The rickety contraption begins to rock violently. I fear it is going to topple over and set him free. "Please," I say, "can we just go?"

I toss my bag inside the trunk and wait. Nick hesitates, watching the raccoon struggle. It hurts him to see any animal confined like that, the mental head-beating, the stunning confusion, that pure-white and splitting fear. As a kid, Nick spent too much time alone in the woods. I suspect that this is part of the reason he is so sensitive with animals and entirely distrusting of other human beings. When we go fishing, he does not let me keep any of the fat bass that we collect in the bucket. He insists we return them to the lake at the end of the day. I watch them longingly while I can, wishing I could fillet each one down to its pretty, delicate bones and cook the pearly flesh with lemon and sea grass. Instead, we kiss them each on the mouth and set them free.

Nick is not an only child, but his half brother is nine years older, and was married and out of the house by the time Nick was eight. The nearest potential playmate lived seven miles away. Nick built himself a little cabin just beyond the brush at the edge of his parents' property where he stuffed his *Highlights* magazines into the makeshift mailbox at night. He was invariably delighted to find them there in the morning. He occupied himself with long solitary walks, tipping over dead or dying trees, and fishing at David Pond where his parents own a cabin only slightly sturdier than the pine construct Nick made himself. The cabin is twenty miles north of the family home and they spent every summer there since the year Nick turned six. His parents bought two used kayaks and taught both sons how to paddle, and then, as they got older, to glide silently into the lily pads and cast their fishing lines into the shade. They didn't see Nick much after that. He left early in the mornings and only returned after dark, every fish carefully released back into the pond, his small, plump hands sticky with worm guts.

Nick doesn't go to the cabin much anymore, but he wants to take me there on our way up north. We are going to journey from New Hampshire to northern Maine, where I will see my first moose. He has assured me of this. It was a great surprise and he told me quickly and in whispers as we lay on the floor, my unpacked bags tossed in a heap in the living room. I am all smiles, jittery with anticipation. He made plans for us to stay at a little bed-and-breakfast in Oquossoc, Maine. But first to the cabin, which is on our way, where there's a broken window that needs fixing, and Nick can finally clean out the gutters. He can't stop talking about it.

The first time Nick took me to the house he grew up in, I was shocked by the desolation of the town. I felt safe, though, and out of the way, as if I were stepping outside the current of time and watching my real life speed by without me—free to fall, free to smash into rocks. However it pleased.

By August the pastures are cleared, the hills rusted orange at their edges, as if by their proximity to the sun. The only neighbors are a family of farmers who live across the street. They raise turkeys that wander into his parents' yard, poking their prehistoric faces into the bathroom window, which is low to the ground. Turkeys are very curious, unlike the chickens that huddle in tight congregations and squawk obscenities when I pass, no doubt sensing my urban beginnings—the particularly hurried gait. No, I am not interested in chickens, nor in raccoons. What I really want to see is a moose, to feel dwarfed by its immensity, to feel powerless and inconsequential, like Nick when he first came to Philadelphia and spent an entire afternoon gazing up at the skyscrapers.

I remember once reading a Cree legend about a grandmother who is also a moose. She gives her own two shinbones to her human grandson to use as ice picks during his travels, so that he can climb mountains. I think Nick would hand over his shinbones, too, but I'll never ask. And maybe that is why I've come so far from home, from the scarred concrete streets of Philadelphia, to this quiet university in New

Hampshire. Because the people I love keep dying, or else they are drowning in grief, and there is too much responsibility in all that grieving. It is selfish, I know, but I am learning to forgive myself. I left the place where people need me, and I need them, and I'm climbing mountains in this new relationship with a solid, healthy man from Maine. We are only a year old together, all animal instinct, and he still handles me like I am of a rare and reckless breed, like something that might take off running with the next rustle in the trees. And, truly, I might. This new consistency can be unnerving.

"Yeah, we can go," Nick says, staring at the raccoon, his eyes narrowed, his hips squared and set north.

By the time we reach the family cabin on David Pond it is a shivering dawn. The trees are heavy with snow and droopy like sulking children. The car crunches over rocks and dirt and I am not entirely sure that we are going the right way, but it is not a good time to argue. Neither of us has slept. The pond looks more like a lake to me, but I don't push this anymore. Nick says my idea of a lake is the "disease-infested cesspools peddling as swimming pools just off city side streets." I don't tell him that as kids, my brother and I weren't allowed to swim in public pools, so we splashed around in fountains instead, picking up pennies with our toes and listening for the ice cream truck.

"I found my Dad in one of those once," I say. "He was floating on one of those pool rafts with his work boots still on."

We pull into the driveway and Nick turns off the car. I feel the cold immediately, like a swift slap to the face. The passenger window in Nick's old Toyota never closes all the way.

"Was he drunk?" he says after a while.

"I don't think so. He just looked tired. I was rushing home from school and didn't stop to ask."

"Well," he says.

We sit in the car for many minutes, too tired to move. The sun breaks over the frozen pond, catching in the cracks like flames. Nick closes his eyes and leans back against the headrest. I watch clumps of snow slip from the elbows of tree branches and tumble to the ground, breaking apart as they fall, disintegrating in the colorless light. I feel heavy. A wet cold is snaking around my ankles. There is a piece of cloud in my eye and a liquor burn on my lips. The cabin is behind us, and in my half-sleep I leave my body and move toward the shore. I reach under the snow and pick clean the bones that peek out of the dirt, fingering the joints that fall apart in my hands. These are old graves and they threaten to split wide and pull me under; the moonless current is strong here. I see Nick from a great distance, that gentle soul, a boy really, snoring lightly, disturbing no one. I want to keep moving, always, but I know we need to rest.

He opens his eyes. He is watching me. He wipes at my face and pulls me toward him, holding my head to his chest. We don't make it into the cabin. There isn't any heat inside anyway. Every few hours, I hear Nick start the engine and feel the dry heat blowing on my neck.

We sleep like this for most of the morning, and then make sandwiches with the white bread and lunchmeat he packed in a cooler.

We sing as we drive—a song we make up about moose. *Going on a moose hunt . . .* That's all we have, so we sing this chorus over and over and dance wildly in our seats, beating time on the dashboard. We lost radio reception a while back, soon after we pulled away from the cabin. Before we left, Nick filled three black trash bags with the wet leaves from the gutters while I carefully pulled large sections of broken glass from a splintered window frame, flakes of white paint disappearing in the snow. I watched Nick as he nailed a thin piece of plywood over the window hole, his face flushed and his tongue hanging out like it does when he is concentrating. He is thin but solid, and he moves with such willfulness that I almost stumble or weep, so earnest is that man, so devoid of all my prickly cynicism.

Now, we are moving on. We are looking for moose. Waves of shadow skip across the highway in front of us. A squirrel runs into the middle of the road, trembles, then darts for the bushes. Afternoon dissolves silently into dusk, bowing and graceful as she slinks off to bed. I am eating a banana I bought at a gas station five miles back. Eventually, we grow sick of singing about moose and begin to sing about bananas.

Nick assures me that we will see a moose in Oquossoc, at a place called the Height of the Land, a scenic outpost that overlooks Mooselookmeguntic Lake.

"*Moose-look-at-me-guns, chick,*" he calls it. "How can we go wrong?"

I am not convinced. It is too late in the season and our odds aren't good, according to the bearded man at the gas station. I don't know why, but I trust a man with a beard when it comes to moose, I tell Nick, and he shrugs and rolls his eyes, rubbing his smooth chin and scowling.

"The moose is the symbol of self-esteem," Nick says. "You could learn something from a moose."

He eats a handful of Swedish Fish and offers me the bag. There's one left so I bite its head off.

"When you see one, it means you are confronting all the various planes of existence between the self and the environment."

"Do you believe that?" I ask.

"Of course not, but doesn't it sound sexy?"

"Absolutely," I say, feeding him the tail.

I study the map, run my finger west along the red highway line until I find Oquossoc. Then I keep going—past Wilson's Mills, over the Canadian border and into Quebec, north to Montreal, then to a place called Saint-Sauveur-des-Monts (*what might that be like?*), and on past recognition. I suppose we could eat grilled cheese sandwiches at a roadside diner in Saskatchewan and a man called Griz might teach us to play five-card stud, beating us every time. We could see a moose rise from the banks of Utikuma Lake like a past life, shaking off silver water slicks like bad memories. He will turn and look at us with quiet absolution as we drive on across Canada—into Alaska, perhaps, over breakneck mountain passes so clean, so rich, we eat dinner and pick our teeth with pine needles.

At last, we might come to our new home, a cozy place with a garden on the edge of everything, on a tiny teardrop of land that dangles in Norton Bay, which I imagine is haggard and bold and indifferent.

Here is a truth: I cry only when we make love.

"I know," he says quietly. "It's okay."

I pull at the flounced curtains beside the bed, tucking my head inside them to stare through the window at the falling snow. Nick pulls me back onto the bed and wraps me up in the floral polyester blanket that scratches my bare skin and makes me laugh a bit too maniacally. He stares at me with concern. And so does that deer, whose tattered head hangs on the wall across from the bed, and who was witness to the whole routine—Nick's round freckled back and the soles of my chapped feet making slow circles in the air. The fervent harmonies, the two pallid asses, and that final black wall that I beat with my fists until it lets me in, tired and defeated, crying helplessly on a concrete floor. In those moments, Nick is gone. I am alone, as I should be, and I feel like maybe I will cry forever. My body does not seem to know the difference between ecstasy and death, joy and pain, and I begin to wonder if they are just the same after all. Like energy, the needle vibrates whether the source is light or sound. When I cry, I suspect it has everything to do with the dead father, absent so long and then poof, *auf wiedersehen*, the week before my eighteenth birthday. Then, my sudden departure from Philadelphia, from my home, with all that sadness and mortality trailing behind me like the train of a wedding gown I can't take off. Or else it is because, in those moments, I am gone, and I'm not yet confident that this man will still be here when I get back. It is the loss of control that terrifies me.

WE MET NANCY, the owner of this bed-and-breakfast, when we arrived in Oquossoc this afternoon. She is big-haired and ebullient. We are her first guests in many weeks and she is delighted to have us. She offers us dinner: tomato salad and a spicy chili with cornbread. Afterward, we sit by the fire and play Scrabble and I win, which means Nick has to call my mother "just to chat." Nancy is watching *Wheel of Fortune* in another room. I can hear the clicking of the wheel while the contestants demand "Big money!" and Pat Sajak orders Vanna to "Show us an M!" and the crowd cheers wildly.

My mother answers and Nick says, "Hi, Susan!" too eagerly, squinting his eyes at me and frowning, so I know she is drunk.

She's been doing this a lot lately—sitting in front of her computer all night and drinking a bottle or two of red wine. She plays word games and smokes cigarettes, her two dogs panting at her feet and walking in circles.

It's not me she needs. I know that. But I can't help but feel that I should be there with her, watching movies and shoveling her driveway, teasing the swollen tics from the bellies of her dogs and wiping their paws when they come in from the yard. My mother and I grew up together in many ways, waged some of the same vertiginous battles with my father, suffered over my little brother as he grew indignant and square-jawed. *Our son*, she'd sometimes say to me accidentally. *What are we going to do about our son?*

Just as often I feel as helpless as an infant and I wish for my mother, if just to force me out of bed in the morning, pick out my clothes, and make me eat.

Nick is gracious and talks to her for several minutes, as if he does not hear how her tongue has grown thick, the words running together like melting butter. I know that voice well, and after Nick says, "Bye, Susan. Yes, very soon. I miss you, too. Okay. Okay. Uh huh. Okay. Here's Jess," and hands me the phone, I say a few words and hang up quickly.

She is sad because Eric has taken to snorting OxyContin in her bathroom, still lying and stealing and denying in that *same fucking straight-faced way* as the husband once did, until she feels she's gone completely nuts. I know how she feels, and yet I am unable to change it. And maybe Eric is, too.

I get up from bed to wash my face in the bathroom sink. The soaps are shaped like ducklings and clustered in a porcelain nest, which makes me laugh. When I get back, Nick and I lie on separate sides of the bed, wrapped in cocoons of exhaustion. I have already forgotten about my father's death, three years ago now, about the amorphous desolation he's left in his stead, about the spectacle I keep making of myself, and the tender way Nick sometimes presses on my chest, as if to soothe away the pain there, whispering, "Let it out, it's okay. You can let it out." My grief is childlike and pure and has little to do with the father himself—he only represents the incompleteness I feel, my own wretchedness. I feel my mind clamoring desperately to reclaim the higher consciousness of youth, those swift and heartbreaking moments of clarity that I lost forever on the day he fell down those stairs, seizing, and his bowel burst and shit poisoned his blood, already thin with booze, and his heart stopped, simple as that.

A blue-fanged raccoon chases me down to the riverbanks of consciousness, where I wake in a sweat and tangled in blankets. Nick is packing his suitcase in the flickering glow of the muted television, and I realize he is leaving me here, naked in this damp dark, my legs still half-buried in the alluvium. *This was inevitable*, I think. *He's finally had it with the theatrics. The melancholy that comes on like a tidal wave. The way I always want to eat at restaurants and hate to cook. The birthmark on my back that looks like a melting snowman. And how I never manage to remember which of his nieces is Courtney, and which is Britney.* It could be any of these things or something else entirely; I know so little of myself sometimes. What I know so completely, in those first dusky moments after waking, is that this is a good, good man and I am sorry to see him go.

He turns and sees me watching, then leaps on the bed like a child on Christmas morning. He pulls back my eyelids with one hand and pinches my nose with the other.

"Wake up, chicken butt," he coos.

He wears a grin of boyish mischief, his blue eyes stained pink from lack of sleep. He grabs a cup of hot coffee from the nightstand and holds it to my lips, the way you do for the infirm. I sip gratefully.

"I wish I had eyelashes as long and dark as yours," I tell him. "It's a waste on boys."

"I wish I had boobs like yours," he says. "I'd play with them all day." He cocks his head to the side, just now considering the implications. "Well, maybe not."

Outside, a pitching snow fills the windows. It is still night, or somewhere in the slim fissure just before dawn, and dark branches slap against the glass. I feel a survivor's exultation.

"Get up," he says. "Put on a sweatshirt."

I move slowly, clutching the coffee mug like a life preserver. If I let go, I'm going back down. I see that it is four in the morning, the witching hour if ever there was one. I grab my jacket and put on socks, padding behind him into the blinding hallway. There is music, I swear, and I hesitate, leaning in toward the wall, aware only of the flowered wallpaper, thousands of tiny lilies raining to the floor.

"What the hell is that?" I say.

"Nancy's playing the piano. She does it every morning. I told her it wouldn't bother us. We were getting up early anyway."

"Of course you did," I say, and he pulls me into the dining room and down the steps and out onto the terrace.

I'm not even resisting this, I realize suddenly, as the snow smacks my cheeks and the freezing wind drags me away from the edge of sleep. Nick is talking, but the blasts of wind are so loud I can't hear him. His lips seem to be moving in slow motion.

"There," he might be saying, pointing out over the hills.

To the south the sky is colorless and the land behind this frozen air is metallic and drained. Suddenly everything feels sped up, like a cartoon, which makes me gasp for air and grab instinctively for the terrace railing, my mug dropping into the snow and disappearing for good. We shouldn't be here, not now, as the empty sky beats back a silver sun and the dead trees draw arrows for the stars. I think I see a figure in the distance, his long stringy legs braced against a slanting mountain bluff, two giant, splintering shinbones thrust like javelins into the ice. I pray, *Don't let go.* I look for Nick, but he is at the bottom of a deep centrifuge, smiling up at me from a long time ago.

"There!" he calls out clearly, suddenly.

I see the black moose ambling out from behind a cluster of bushes, like a piece of night sky shaken loose. My heart stills. He is the distance of a football field away. The moose chews calmly on the spindly branch of a chrysanthemum, stamping his great hoofs in the snow. He extends his neck against the wind and then whips his head forward, tearing platinum gashes in the dark with his enormous antlers. From where we stand, he walks the horizon—one misstep, I think, and he'll fall from the earth's rim, crashing through the universe and bellowing out to the passing galaxies. I walk toward him slowly. I don't want to scare him off. My feet are numb, the snow up to my knees. I imagine reaching out and stroking the coarse fur on his back, clumps of it snapping off like icicles in my hands and falling to the ground. I want to bury my face in his flank and press hard; I want to be inside where it is warm. I imagine the beast reaching back and softly nuzzling me on, snorting impatiently. I take a few tentative steps.

Nick squeezes my hand, checking, and I squeeze back. I've forgotten everything that's come before.

SHE
FEEDS
THEM

GEORGIA STILL MOVES at great speeds, talks too fast, spills secrets as often as the tiny plastic cups of tartar sauce that dress the fried fish as it flies from the kitchen. Steaming heaps of haddock, clams, golden scallop nuggets, and one, two sprigs of fresh parsley. These are family recipes all, family business, and Georgia tends her post at The Crab Shack with the sharp eye of a ship's captain and the intuitive gut-love of a mother. They find her six days a week, twelve hours a day, their prodigal daughter returned, and she feeds them. The customers are nearly all local, loyal, as attached to the woman who runs the place as they are to the grease bed of shucked oysters and oversized onion rings. Her brother, Abram, does the cooking along with Georgia's two grown sons, Michael and Colin. For the four years I spent at the University of New Hampshire, I've been their only waitress—a feckless college kid with graceless speed.

Georgia left Portsmouth, New Hampshire, for the first time at twenty, moved to Reno, Nevada, and married Tim Tally, giving birth to two boys within a year and a half. This was 1983 and Georgia had been waiting tables at her parents' restaurant since she was twelve and precocious, a brown bobble of curls and courtesy—a small-town pride and joy. She fed them and they missed her.

Georgia is a recovering methamphetamine addict. At the time of my employment, she had been clean for eleven years.

"I was one of those housewives that vacuumed for hours, zipping around like a wind-up toy. You know the kind," she said.

But I didn't, could not imagine hours of vacuuming. Her graying dark hair came loose from the ponytail, tight curls floating down her back, coating her white collared shirt in stray strands. She was always losing hairs, pens, thoughts. This is what we did at night after long shifts: I ate a salad with scallops and had a glass of wine. Georgia didn't drink, but she talked and smoked pot and talked some more.

"I was addicted to meth for twelve years," she said one night.

She swept one hand over the table, wiping bits of fried breading onto the floor. Her hands were swollen, masculine, knuckles large and chapped, nails bitten into straight lines.

"Tim Tally worked long days," she said, "came home, fucked me, went to bed after four glasses of Jack Daniel's. I was up all night doing bumps, baking peanut butter cookies, throwing them out and starting over, rocking babies back to sleep."

He was always "Tim Tally." Never just "Tim" or "Timothy" or "Mr. Tally." I pictured him ruddy-faced and bowlegged and donning a suede cowboy hat.

Georgia has been back in Portsmouth for ten years, having answered the request of her brother, Abram, and her Greek Orthodox parents. They had pleaded with their recovering daughter to bring their grandsons home, to "leave that Tim Tally and his drugs, that barren soil and those wasted, amoral Southwesterners." They had sucked her in, fed on her "good, Greek brain," her "healthy Mediterranean spirit." "Come home, Georgia. Come home and help your brother in the restaurant." Eventually, she did—a slow, medicated flight over a shifting American landscape, greens and browns and beiges melting together and then apart, as if separated by a centrifuge. She thought those magnificent colors were as close to God as she would ever get. She watched with her forehead pressed to the small, rectangular window and fielded tugs from small boys who climbed over their mother's lap, their little, restless fingers wound tightly into her mass of curly hair. She was thirty-eight and had been sober for nearly a year.

During the four years of my tenure, the routine at The Crab Shack rarely changed. On Mondays, Tuesdays, and Wednesdays, I came in for a few hours after my classes to work the dinner shift, and I returned on weekend mornings to work lunch. Her sons, both in their early twenties now, clanged around in the kitchen until well after the last customers were gone and the tables reset. They scrubbed pots and scraped the shimmery flakes of fish skin from the cutting boards, Led Zeppelin or Neil Young playing on an old boom box. On the few nights when I left alone through the darkened kitchen, the moon slid through the open door and caught on the stray scales scattered over every surface like silver drift snow. In the stark light of day, though, they were mostly invisible. The dining room disappeared when Abram flipped the last light switch.

"Get your purse from the office. I'm locking up," Georgia would say, and then evaporate (or so it seemed) through the heavy swinging doors and into the kitchen's blinding lights and cold steel fluorescence. She would share a quick joint with her son, Michael, and then stomp down the stairs and into the office.

"Smoke 'em if you got 'em!" she might yell out.

In the mornings, we started again. I vacuumed without enthusiasm and Georgia set the tables with blue paper placemats and bendable silverware, water glasses still warm from the dishwasher. She buffed each one before setting it down on the top right corner of the placemat. She filled salt and pepper shakers to the tip-top and ran a damp rag over dustless window sills. Downstairs, Michael slipped cans of Bud or Bud Light into his jacket pocket to have during his lunch break and occasionally I found a warm Sam Adams stuffed into my purse at the end of the night. This I would drink gratefully during my walk home.

At ten to eleven every morning, Frank Hurley is always at the door waiting for Georgia to flip the sign and let him in.

"Mr. Hurley, how are you?" Georgia says.

She smiles and strides over to where the old man is standing. He wavers slightly as he drags one heavy foot after the other through the door. She takes his arm and helps him to his table, always number five, always the first to be seated on a Saturday. He throws his jacket into the booth and slides to the wall next to the window so he can watch for his brother. I come to know the idiosyncrasies of so many customers. I work five days a week, and in that time the customers at The Crab Shack become as comfortable and predictable as the woman who feeds them. Georgia knows all of their stories, when wives died and children graduated, when jobs were lost and legs broken and mortgages paid in full, their favorite sexual appetites, and the salad dressings they prefer. She brings the old man his cranberry tea. He sips tentatively for an hour until exactly noon when his brother, Charlie, finally arrives, cane in hand. Charlie has a thin wash of white hair that barely conceals his freckled scalp and the scabs from run-ins with doorframes. Though Charlie is younger than Frank, he looks much older. He spent his life scraping asbestos from the peeling walls and crumbling ceilings of tenement apartments in Boston.

While her parents are in Florida, six months of every year, Georgia sleeps in their bed, watches movies on cable television (she doesn't have cable in her own apartment), works six days of every week, and never goes out. She talks on the phone to her only friend, Mitch, who still lives alone in Arizona and keeps various shotguns hidden in his empty mansion. Georgia's parents' house is midway between Portsmouth, New Hampshire, and Kittery, Maine, and Georgia and the boys share an apartment below the main house where her parents live. Michael and Colin are grateful when their mother stays upstairs. They drink beers together and arrive at work early or right on time. They, too, seldom go out. Colin makes some exceptions for his dates, though most often the girls must come to his house. They are sweet and courteous boys and often step out from the kitchen to shake hands and say hellos, first wiping their fingers on tattered white aprons.

"How'd they end up so normal?" Georgia wondered one night, staring at the maroon wall that separates the dining room from the kitchen where her sons scrub black grime from pots and pans, their aprons soaked through with grease and butter and the liquefied fat from salmon fillets.

Both boys are handsome, though Colin is the better looking of the two. He dates often, unlike his older brother, Michael, whose one brown eye floats away lazily if he's not paying attention or if he's paying too much attention, while the other eye remains locked in place. They are dark-haired and skinny and smile easily. They call Georgia "Mommy" without any hint of embarrassment and sneak her kisses when it's not too busy.

"I never had big goals," said Georgia. "I just always wanted to be a mother, ever since I was a little girl. That's it. I just wanted to be a mother."

"And now you are," I said.

"People need me. It feels good to be needed," she said.

I asked her if being needed made her happy. She said she thought she was as happy as she'd ever get. She folded a placemat into a paper airplane and added it to the collection next to the register. Each one was different. Some had colored wings, red or blue crayon designs, or little pilots that looked like Martians.

"I feel just like a teenager sometimes," she said softly. "Like they should be raising me."

She gestured toward the kitchen where her boys were cleaning up. Since she began attending Narcotics Anonymous meetings, Georgia learned that drugs like meth stunt you emotionally.

"That's why I act like I'm twenty," she said. "You're left *just* where you were when you took to the drug."

I asked her how a twenty-year-old could run a successful restaurant, raise two great kids, and tend to a small town like the local therapist or mayor.

"Well, what else?" she said, as if the script wasn't hers to rewrite.

The boys stumbled out from the kitchen and tossed their dirty aprons onto the counter, sliding into the booth next to Georgia and me. She patted their chests and kissed each cheek as they grinned and leaned away, tipping back full beers and picking at their fingernails.

"Up," she said, and they slid out of the booth so Georgia could make them salads and chicken fingers tossed with spicy buffalo sauce, her own secret recipe.

They ate without looking up. Georgia puffed on her bowl of pot and smiled at them. The dishwasher finally stopped its clacking.

The last time I saw Georgia was the day she fired me. She left me a clipped message on my answering machine after I overslept and missed our first staff meeting. I was devastated, inconsolable. I ran the twelve blocks down to The Crab Shack in just my sweatpants and a T-shirt. It was the middle of February and I remember the hairs on my arms standing straight up as I ran, my shoelaces slapping against the sidewalk. When I burst into the restaurant, Georgia was at the register and I could see Abram peeking out from the kitchen, his hand hovering over a plate of pink uncooked fish. I looked at Georgia and we both started to cry—ugly, choking sounds that startled the customers. She took off, slamming the kitchen door behind her. I gave chase. She had been my friend and I felt betrayed. I was also embarrassed for missing the meeting and this made me cry harder, like a child who falls off a chair and cries from humiliation rather than pain. Inside the kitchen, Michael caught my arm while Georgia slipped out the back door. I knew she regretted her decision and I wanted to grab her shoulders and make her say so, hold her thick hair in my fist and force a confession, demand her love, steal her good graces. I was that kind of kid. I couldn't stand to be disliked and I'd never before confronted anyone about anything.

"She feels like she's losing control," Michael said to me. "She's making an example out of you. There's nothing we could say."

He was talking to me but staring at my chin, the one wayward eyeball bobbing helplessly toward the door. The lights flickered and Abram banged on the metal freezer to make them stop.

"She threatened to leave," Michael said.

He let go of me and wiped his nose with the back of his hand. "She wants to move to Arizona." He blinked rapidly several times in a row.

I remembered Georgia once telling me how the doctor had forbade Michael from ever drinking again. How he had told him that one more drink would kill him, a complication of his severe epilepsy, and how later Michael had stood outside the doctor's office slurping from a can of warm Budweiser he'd gotten from his trunk and kicking at the wall, beer foam sliding down his chin. Georgia had to drag him into the car and lock the doors. "Even then, he cracked the windshield and shook like a yearling all the way home," she'd whispered.

"We had to give her something," Michael said. "She needed to feel in control."

Truth is, I was never a very good waitress. I didn't care much that Joe Ruggle liked his scallops well done, that Coach Warner liked his Diet Coke in a wine glass. Years later, I'll get fired from another restaurant for pouring the wrong year to a "very important" customer, and decide to quit the industry for good. But Georgia pays attention to these details. They matter to her. "People come to The Crab Shack because they crave it," she said once. "It's no fun satisfying a craving unless it's *just right*. Besides, there are enough disappointments in life. You might as well have a good dinner."

I closed my eyes. When I opened them again Michael was peeling a shrimp. I turned around and walked back through the restaurant toward the front door. Mr. Hurley looked up from his plate of broiled haddock but I couldn't stop. As I was leaving, the door flew open from the wind and I heard the telephone ringing and ringing.

IN
NEW YORK

IN NEW YORK, I am twenty-two and learning how to be a teacher with other twenty-two-year-olds. Nick moves with me from New Hampshire after college graduation and we get a small apartment together and play house.

In New York, I am twenty-two and learning how teachers will change the world.

In New York, I stay up all night drinking with a black woman in her thirties who is teaching me how to be a teacher. At dawn, she tells me that she'd thought I was just another precious white girl from the suburbs who thinks she can change the world.

In New York, I stay up all night drinking with a twenty-two-year-old lesbian who thinks she can change the world. At dawn, I beg her to kiss me and she says no.

In New York, I am a teacher. I never thought I could change the world.

In New York, a twelve-year-old boy brings me his drawings every day during my lunch period. I tell him they are wonderful and he should keep drawing. He believes me. They are wonderful, though I'm not sure it matters. But that's not what I tell him.

In New York, I watch a mother beat the shit out of her kid during a parent-teacher conference. I am outraged. I go to the principal and tell her that we have to do something. Just like that: *We have to do something!* I go to the principal and she tells me to calm down. I go to the principal and she tells me to shut up and think. What will happen if we call someone? Do I think the kid will be better off in foster care? "Do you think this will be better for the kid?" she asks. "Think," she says. I go to the principal and she tells me this isn't "happy little white world." I go to the principal and she holds my hand and says, "Just do your job."

In New York, my students write essays about dead parents and drugs.

In New York, I write essays about dead parents and drugs. I don't sleep. I come home and fall on the floor and cry. I never thought I could change the world. I don't know what I thought.

In New York, my seventh-graders read on a first-grade level.

In New York, my students fuck in the bathroom. They throw chalk at me and put each other in choke holds. Together, we play word games and eat candy. We sing songs and have dance-offs. We line up like they tell us to. Other teachers give me dirty looks when my students are not quiet in the halls. Other teachers give me dirty looks when our line is not straight.

In New York, I have a student named Quinesha who gets picked on for being small. She hides under my desk in the mornings and says, "Ain't nobody gonna find me here. Ain't nobody gonna find me here."

In New York, I walk Quinesha home and she tells me I will quit soon. I am quiet, and then I say she can call me anytime.

In New York, I quit three weeks after my conversation with Quinesha. I get a job waiting tables at a little Italian restaurant and do cocaine in the bathroom with my boss. "You could be the manager here," he tells me. "This could be your place soon," he says. Soon, I quit.

In New York, I walk everywhere. I avoid the subway, the bus, the area in Brooklyn where I was once a teacher. I spend a lot of time in Chinatown looking at fish on ice, the slick octopus and the frogs in buckets, heaving. A man yells at me for running my finger over the wet eye of a John Dory. I watch the old men playing checkers in the park. I watch jugglers tossing fire.

In New York, I go to a book festival and sit in the back on the floor at a reading. I have to pee, but I don't want to leave because I'm too excited. The author says he doesn't want to be here. He says his best friend killed himself yesterday and he doesn't want to be here, but he has to. A woman raises her hand and says, "Just leave then."

In New York, I let Nick fuck me in the ass for the first time. We do it on the floor because we don't have a bed yet and I laugh the whole time because it tickles. It really does.

In New York, I exaggerate on my resume and get a job at a fancy, expensive restaurant. I don't make any money, but I wait on people like Leonardo DiCaprio and Beyoncé and Martha Stewart. Well, I don't wait on them, but I bring their food from the kitchen. I meet a girl who says she makes her money in other ways and she will teach me if I want. I think about it. One night the manager gives me $20 because it was so slow and he feels bad for me. He is usually stoic and intimidating and I feel so grateful that I overdo it with the thank yous until he has to tell me to stop talking and go home. Then on New Year's Eve, I make $600 serving the mayor's table. After our shift, we drink all the leftover bottles of Veuve Clicquot and I forget about Nick waiting at home. I come in at five in the morning and he is drunk on the couch; his glasses are crooked, an empty bottle of champagne on the floor. "I thought you were coming home," he says. It's the first time I've seen him drunk and I help him to the bathroom to puke.

In New York, a man on the subway takes his dick out of his pants and presses it against Nick's thigh.

In New York, I go for long runs along the river, but I usually get distracted and stop running halfway through.

In New York, we pay $30 for a Christmas tree that looks like the Charlie Brown tree, one thin crooked trunk and three wimpy branches. We decorate it with old MetroCards and a handful of silver balls from the dollar store. We are overly proud.

In New York, I accidentally kill all the plants on our fire escape.

In New York, I make a million plans to leave New York. I read Gretel Ehrlich and Cormac McCarthy and Joy Williams.

I read Chekhov and Tobias Wolff and Annie Dillard—lots of Annie Dillard. I read about everywhere but New York.

In New York, we take ourselves out to restaurants we can't afford and eat so much we stumble home groaning.

In New York, I get a job at a sports bar and work until four in the morning with girls from all over the world. We take shots all night with the customers and cheer for teams we don't know or care about. We go home with wads of cash tucked into our short shorts. One time I walk home at eight in the morning and it starts to snow and I am so in love with New York in that moment that I start to cry. When I get to the front door of our building, Nick walks up behind me and says he's been looking for me for hours.

In New York, a man tells me I'm "fuckable, but that's about it." He says he is an engineer and he can break my body down to all its parts and put them back together again. He tells me he can do this with his eyes closed. I work with a girl from Spain who tells him to get out. She says *pussy* so that it rhymes with *loosey-goosey* and I fall in love with her a little. We go to Central Park on our day off and lie in the sun topless and drink vodka and orange juice from water bottles.

In New York, I decide to become a vegetarian and it lasts for seven hours.

In New York, I do cocaine with a co-worker from New Zealand on his front stoop. He asks me if I want to move to Japan with him and I say yes, just to see what would happen. Nothing happens.

In New York, I start paying to have my laundry done for me because the way they fold it so neatly and wrap it tightly in shrink-wrap feels like tenderness. Also, because I'm lazy and we live in a fourth-floor walk-up.

In New York, I become obsessed with real estate.

In New York, I get drunk with Nick and we decide we want to have a threesome. We get into a cab and I ask the driver to take us to a lesbian bar and we only realize how ridiculous we are being when we get there. By the time we get home, I'm too tired to fuck anyway.

In New York, I get an apartment by myself north of Manhattan in Yonkers. I start graduate school. Nick moves away to start graduate school somewhere else. We visit each other on the weekends and have hard, hungry sex.

In New York, my landlords are an older Italian couple and they live above me. They are in their sixties and their grown son lives in the basement. On Sundays, the husband brings me fresh olive bread and the newspaper. He brings me dark plums from the backyard and balls of mozzarella that are still warm. He leaves these things in paper bags on my doorstep and knocks and runs away. I love him so much it hurts. The one time I have a friend over he leaves a pizza and a Post-it Note that reads "For you eat your friends."

In New York, the husband wraps the plum trees in cheese-cloth for the winter. He is short and stout and looks up at me with his chin tucked into his neck. He has bright blue eyes and frowns, but it doesn't mean he's unhappy. That's just his face.

In New York, the husband is a barber and a casino pit boss. He works all the time. His wife wishes they could take a vacation, but they never do. He can't sit still. He mows the yard and plants flowers and weeds the garden and rakes the leaves and walks up and down the street clearing the snow from neighbors' driveways. He works from six in the morning until ten at night, every day except Sunday. The wife asks if I will write about them someday.

In New York, the Italian couple invites me up for dinners. They think I don't eat enough. They feed me olives and pickled mushrooms and breaded veal. They feed me radicchio salads and hard cheeses and soft cheeses and cheeses so pungent they smell like farm animals and hay. They feed me fat grapes with seeds and watermelon and sliced tomatoes. They feed me the wine that the husband makes in the garage and I like the way he drinks it, by pouring single gulps into a mason jar and slugging them back, then pouring again. They feed me coffee so strong and bitter it clears my nasal passages.

In New York, I ask the husband to be the subject of an oral history project for a class I'm taking in graduate school. We sit for hours at his kitchen table and I record him talking about growing up in Italy during the war. He tells me about making bread out of chestnuts and sleeping with hot bricks by his feet. He teaches me how to tell stories. He gives me all of his family photos to scan. He takes me to the first places he lived when he got to the States. I make a video of him showing me these row homes in the Bronx and the tiny delis on Arthur Avenue and the parks where he spent most of his time. He tells me about

Tar Beach, the rooftops where they would set up chairs and blankets in the summer. He tells me he will take me to the San Gennaro festival in Little Italy in September. He tells me he will take me mushroom hunting in the fall.

In New York, they fight so loudly that the walls vibrate. It makes me feel less lonely when they fight.

In New York, I invite his whole family to the end-of-the-year exhibition where everyone in the class puts their projects on display. I work day and night for months to put my video project together and I am proud and nervous and want to give back just a little of what he has given to me. He seems reluctant, but he agrees to come. He asks if he will have to answer questions. He takes off work. The whole family shows up and he is wearing a jacket and tie. The room is crowded and people wander around looking at our work. I put in the DVD of my project and it doesn't work, not one bit of it. It never copied onto the disc. I run to the bathroom and throw up in the toilet. They are sweet. They say they understand. They leave early.

In New York, I make more plans to leave New York. On moving day, the husband says he knows I'll come back. He says I can live in my little apartment for free. He says I am like a daughter. The wife makes me a plate of food to go. He whispers, "You'll come back."

But I don't go back. It's too hard. Nick and I will spend a couple of years in Connecticut and I'll teach college writing to freshman while he does research in New Haven. Then, he'll get a job at the University of Vermont and I won't get a job, not right away, but I'll move to Vermont with him and write all day.

Many months later, I drive down from Connecticut and drop a copy of Dante's *Inferno* in Italian into the couple's mailbox because the husband once mentioned that he'd like to read it. Once, I stop by the barbershop when I'm driving through, but he isn't there. Once, I have a dream that they nurse me back to health. Once, I plant a plum tree in my new backyard in Vermont, but it doesn't take. Once, I try to call, but only once.

**IF ONLY
YOU PEOPLE
COULD
FOLLOW
DIRECTIONS**

THE MOTEL IS flamingo pink, stucco walls dripping with humidity; the whole rectangular complex feels (from the fever, I suppose) like a gaping mouth. I am in the wet center of the mouth, floating in a pool of tepid water and staring up at the rain clouds that rush by. The muscular white sun squeezes my head like a stress ball. My mother smears cream cheese onto a bagel at the wobbly glass table next to the pool and worries aloud about my brother, Eric, alone in our motel room.

It is August 2010, and this is Delray Beach, Florida, a place inundated with recovery homes and so-called pain clinics, "pill mills" manned by crooked doctors profiting from an epidemic of pain-killer addiction. Together, the homes and the clinics are a self-sustaining economy, trading the addicts back and forth like playing cards. Of course, this is all on the periphery, away from the bustling downtown and its many moneyed tourists. My mother and I are visiting Eric, who has been in a recovery home here for the past nine months, or so we had thought.

The whole place seems tuned to a higher decibel than up north. I feel accosted by the neon colors and blaring trumpet solos, frenetic sound bites from a nearby highway. Even the foliage seems offensive. The leaves are as big as platters and so bright I have to squint to differentiate one from another. This giant palm just might, any second now, slap me in the face. I hear a faint sizzle as I dip my head in and out of the water. A circle of light has caught a chameleon capering around a drainpipe. Curtains wave and then draw open on the third floor.

This is not the first time I have gotten sick in anticipation of seeing my brother. I have a friend who calls me *unbalanced*, always with an apologetic grin. I do not argue—unless, of course, I have not been taking my Lexapro. Then I argue a lot. As a family, we have a habit of seeking each other out at just the wrong time, when one of us or all of us are about to go over the deep end. My mother, my brother, and me. This reminds me of the way my extended family tends to gather only for funerals. We do a lot of sitting around and eating. Storing up, I suppose, for what will seem a long winter's chill.

A yellow beetle floats past my cheek before getting tangled in my hair. I watch sidelong with one eye shut as the beetle does a frantic doggy paddle. I imagine myself in the ocean caught in a bed of cloying, endless black kelp, choking and sputtering, a monstrous pale hand suddenly wrenching me free, tossing me across millions of miles of space into a different hemisphere, a different planet, then a second of shimmering exultation before the break.

"I hid my Ativan in the curtains," my mother says, chewing. "You think he'll find it there?"

"Absolutely," I say. I float over to the steps and open my mouth, hoping she'll stick that bagel inside.

She does.

Though we didn't know it until we arrived in Florida, Eric was kicked out of the recovery home six months ago after relapsing on OxyContin. The cops searched his car outside of a 7-Eleven after a friend was caught trying to swipe a seven-dollar bottle of sparkling rosé. Since then, he's been living with his girlfriend, Adrienne, in her college dorm room, where they like nothing better than to huddle together on the bottom bunk, tie each other off, and shoot bumps of liquefied Oxy into their skinny arms, those bubblegum-blue veins.

In other words, our trip was planned as a happy reunion, a celebration of nine months of sobriety, which is partially what I mean when I say we are tragically, cosmically, bound.

But I can't help imagining this small, pretty girl laying her head on my brother's birdy chest as he smacks her forearm and fingers a vein, grinning like a schmuck as he loads the needle. He is twenty-three and she is twenty. They have dark hair and gangly legs and heavy eyebrows. Seeing them together, you would think *they* were siblings. They both walk a bit bow-legged and laugh in the same reckless way, heads tossed to the sky. They sometimes speak in tongues, it seems, and communicate with small, almost indecipherable, gestures.

On our first night in Florida, before we knew he'd been kicked out of the recovery home, my mother and I picked them up from a corner store and took them to an Italian restaurant where Eric had recently worked and been quickly fired. Watching them across the table, I felt a moment of jealousy, such was their intimacy. In comparison, Nick and I look like the couple in the painting *American Gothic*, while Eric and Adrienne are Bonnie and Clyde. I mourned the days when my brother and I were in cahoots, sneaking joints on the back porch as teenagers, and earlier still, conspiring to get out of trouble. Eric can talk his way out of anything, but I anticipate my mother's needs like no one else. *Coffee?* I'd offer at dawn every Christmas morning. There is a picture of me as proof: three years old, wearing a blue beaded bikini, and lighting my mother's cigarette.

There was a time, when we were teenagers, when our favorite topic of conversation was how we could, if need be, get away with murder. I remember it involved shaving ourselves head to toe and a lot of scattering of parts.

"Hey! Remember how we'd kill people?" I blurted out at the Italian restaurant. "I mean, how we could, you know, if we ever had to, like, get away with it?" My brother looked at me, confused, his hand shaking as he put down his forkful of spaghetti. Eric's girl didn't seem to hear, but kept shoveling lasagna past her plump lips, color slowly filling her cheeks. Our mother laughed too loud.

"Oh, *God*," she groaned.

"I guess so," Eric said, and I was, for a second, embarrassed and a little pissed off. It made me think of the family of stray cats near my home in Connecticut, where Nick and I moved after graduate school. They are each orange-and-black striped, with nubby, deformed tails like rudders that shake quickly back and forth when they dart across my back porch chasing squirrels. One of the cats, the runt I call Shitpoke, watches me through the glass door on the porch and takes off if I look up from my coffee, which I try not to do, preferring our feigned disinterest. I don't have many admirers after all.

Eric's dismissal made me feel like one of the squirrels then— run down by some underweight mutant cat with half a tail, one dismembered paw tossed next to the cellar door.

I chew the bagel, wishing I were the type to lose my appetite with sickness. I am not. "Eating, *again?*" my mother likes to say. When Eric called me from a pay phone the morning of our flight to Florida, I knew from his voice that he was using again, which was not part of my plan. I shoveled down two bowls of half-frozen beef stew before collapsing back into bed.

When I had made the drive from Connecticut down to my mother's house in Philadelphia I had been hopeful. Against my better judgment, I thought he was clean. To celebrate, my mother and I got drunk on ten-dollar bottles of wine and I woke up with a fever. That's when Eric called.

We are an imperfect people, full of contradictions. *Do as I say, not as I do*—that sort of thing. Outsiders see me as the most put together, but I harbor a secret: I am just better at faking it. I make it through the day.

Still, we sit and wait and wait. We are in a duel and this is a standstill. Or, we are in a play and rehearsing the same scene for the gazillionth time.

Mother and sister wait outside anxiously while son/brother gets high in tacky Florida motel room/mother's unfinished attic/dimly lit McDonald's bathroom/snow-heavy parked car/bowling alley urinal/ New York City diner/empty New Jersey lifeguard station/suburban basement/family friend's gold-trimmed bathroom/bathroom/bathroom/ bathroom/small black space of empty and release.

Cut.

Take gazillion and one.

This time with a little less weepy-weepy, please. A little less improvisation. A little less lip. A little more faith. A little more higher power. A little more prayer, a little less wine. Cut the crap. Cut the line. Tuck the chin. Look left, right, faster, slower. Pick seven dandelions on the first day of spring. Hate less or more. Work harder. Chew slower. Be better. Look to god, God, GOD. Watch your language. Watch your back. Collect rocks. Lick 'em clean. Count the pigeons in the backyard and multiply times forever. Give it up, let it go, take it back, take control. Say yes. Say no. Say no, no, no. Stick to the script. Steps One through Twelve. One through Twelve. Keep coming back. It works if you work it.

If only you people could follow directions.

When Eric was an infant we rode in my father's pickup truck to an emergency room near Sacramento. He had a fever so high he left red blooms on my mother's thighs where she held him down. I sat between my parents picking at my scratchy big-girl underwear. Eric raged until he went limp, his fat little legs kicking back the tule fog that swallowed the night. My mother was twenty-six. My father was a drunk. I didn't know enough to be afraid, but I remember that dense gray fog reflecting back the dimmed headlights. We made it to the hospital and my father and I left them there for three days. My brother's feet swelled up like little blue loaves of sourdough. The nurse who had improperly inserted his PICC line refused to remove it. "You do it," she told my mother, and left. When my mother refused to quit sobbing another nurse came in, fixed the PICC line, and deposited two yellow pills onto the table.

"I can't give you anything to calm you down," she said, "but I can leave it here."

Our mother used to say that Eric entered the world screaming and didn't stop for an entire year. When I was three, that's all he was to me: a bundle of torrential sound.

When he finally went quiet, I could look at him for hours. Then I knew—I loved him best of all.

Still wet from the pool, I crawl under the polyester blanket and wait for Eric to get out of the bathroom. The sun torches the tiny room and laughs—the Ubiquitous Chuckler, the Convivial Scorcher. *Your name in lights!* The scratch of the fibers against my burning legs is both the best and worst sensation, like picking a scab, like snorting a pill.

"Man, my poop is magic," Eric says, coming into the bedroom and wiping his face with a towel. "It never smells!" Instantly, I see through the line and he sees that I see it, see the whole scene played out like the seventh deadly sin, because I am either destroyed or relieved to have my suspicions confirmed. If he is still getting high, I can still be the good and grieving sibling. Even (dare I say it?) the "favored" child, the dutiful one, the angel to his devil, graced by the glory of genetics, that dark and taciturn wellspring of mysterious fortune, mightier than any god I know. If I keep playing my role, does he have any choice but to keep playing his?

Line?

"You've been in that bathroom for twenty minutes. You're telling me it doesn't smell like shit?"

"What are you trying to say?"

WHEN ERIC WAS four, he fell backward down a flight of stairs inside our grandparents' house and cracked his head open on a giant ceramic monkey with black marbles for eyes. I watched as he fell, curious. I was six. His mouth was a big red O that chewed my heart out. He didn't make a sound. There was a lot of blood, but the monkey didn't flinch. After everyone left for the hospital, I tried to crack the monkey's head with my shoe. *Bad monkey.* Eric got stitches and let me trace them lightly with my finger. I remember being amazed that a head could be held together with just some black thread. Also, I remember that phrase, *cracked his head open*, which the grownups repeated, and which seemed both more and less than what really happened. Sharper than a blow, say, or a thump. Something razor-edged and irreparable. Cracks are small and insidious, the start of some unforeseen disaster, like the fissures in the earth's surface from which volcanoes erupt, craggy and molten. Or even the sidewalk in front of the ShopRite, now upended, churned through with dirt and dry, dead earthworms and rotten tree roots, something to be avoided, circumvented, dangerous. Having been weakened by that first split in his soft skull, it was as if the whole rickety job could come undone at any moment. Still, I loved that phrase and turned it over and over. *Cracked his head open.* I'd once thought that only eggs could be cracked open, and I both thrilled and shuddered at the image of brains, like yolk, oozing out over the floor.

Later that night, my mother and Eric go out to dinner. I stay behind. The fever that started at my mother's house in Philadelphia is swelling behind my eyes, banging on the door. *Shark Week* is on the Discovery Channel, my favorite, except watching *Shark Week* in Florida feels a bit like watching *The Biggest Loser* while gorging on cheeseburgers. Still, the slow switching glide of these silver beasts calms me down. A gray reef shark noses at a clump of coral off the coast of Easter Island. He can't stop moving or he'll drown, the oxygen drawn from the water by thousands of leaflike lamellae in the gills, tiny blood vessels that swell with oxygen as the water passes through. In my real life, the one outside the theater of my brother's addiction, I can't stop moving either: New Hampshire, North Carolina, New York, Connecticut, summers stomping through the Scottish Highlands alone, a pair of blisters belly-up along my heels. I let one of my mother's Ativan dissolve beneath my tongue and hope for sleep. The shark makes a quick dart to the left and then dives headlong into the body of the shadow, propelled by the infinitesimal pulse of an electrical charge that can be, the narrator tells us, as faint as a human heart.

Three years ago, Eric pulled into my mother's driveway in her car. It was three o'clock in the morning and the car was destroyed, the roof folded in on itself like a paper airplane, the windshield and sunroof shattered, snow collecting in the leather seats. He got out and stood in the light of the driveway. Our mother squinted from the porch, her old blue robe wrapped tightly, her arms crossed. As he stumbled toward the door, iridescent glass shards rained from his shoulders onto the blacktop. Blood bubbled from a gash in his forehead. He closed his eyes against the blaze of light from the kitchen window, dropped our mother's keys into her hand, and walked into the house.

My mother called me. It was four o'clock in the morning and I was asleep in my apartment in New York. I heard her dogs barking and my brother screaming in the background. I heard her breathing into the phone. I heard my windowpanes shift to adjust to the rising temperature. I heard the clacking of pipes in the walls and the nearly inaudible click of the earth returning to orbit.

"You fucking cunt!" he yelled. "You fucking self-righteous bitch! This is your fault!" He was out of his head, cracked open, scraped clean. My mother's voice was calm and even and stern. By then, this sort of thing was almost routine.

"I think," she said to me slowly, "I need you to come home. I can't do this one alone."

She gave me the damage report: one stolen credit card, two missing bottles of Ativan (hers and her sister's), a bottle of pain-killers swiped from my grandmother's house, and $200 taken from my grandmother's nightstand. In his pockets, one forged check, two remaining pain-killers, a tiny contraption for grating pills into a fine powder, and one emptied, hollow pen. And of course the stolen car, the keys taken from my mother's purse in the middle of the night. I heard him bellowing wildly from somewhere and my mother hung up the phone.

I drove home. The cold yellow sun spread beyond the city skyline. I drank a thermos of stale coffee. I'd tossed a couple of sweatshirts and a toothbrush onto the back seat, an after-thought. Despite the distance I'd put between myself and my brother, I woke every morning with the fear that this was his last day on earth. The phone call was confirmation that my dread was not unfounded, was maybe even necessary. My dread, I'd thought foolishly, could be a force much stronger than his will. I'd never considered *his* dread, what power that might hold.

By the time I pulled into my mother's driveway I'd for-gotten how I got there. Suddenly I was in her living room drinking coffee. The police were gone. After the accident, miraculously, Eric had only damaged his hand with all the wailing and flinging of his body against walls, the punched holes in his closet door, and the lines of Percocet snorted off an old Fleetwood Mac CD case. He slept and his women drank coffee, called insurance companies, and made plans for the next rehab. He slept and we waited. He slept and we watched.

The fever will soon break, I can tell. I am slick and swollen as a jellyfish, the one Eric sliced open as a kid on the beach with his brand-new Swiss Army knife, tearing through his finger in the process. I saw it happen, all that young blood spilling onto the cool sand. He ran back to our mother, who was sitting in her chair with a book, smoking peacefully. She was the color of cinnamon then, her chest still the palest pink from the blood vessels rupturing there, in slow motion and over time, like exploding stars. As she ages, her chest will turn deep red, a road map of every soothing cigarette. Eric's reaction to his misadventure with the jellyfish was quick, impulsive, and childlike. He buried his knife in the sand and cried out, "The jellyfish bit me! The jellyfish bit me!" My mother sighed and put out her cigarette in the sand and kissed his bleeding pinky. All of that was fine, normal, healthy then. But over the years, Eric's default response to his own behavior remains the same. *It wasn't my fault!* And the lies, so many lies—he believes his own bullshit. Really believes it. *That's the disease talking*, they say, and I try to believe that, too.

For years I believed, but all I see, finally, is my brother's hard familiar face and the illness that my mother continues to try and kiss away with love and money and blunt maternal strength until she, we, are all as sick as Eric—the dead father's legacy, this disease. For a while, I'd felt responsible for Eric's addiction because I handed him pot for the first time, but I realized it would have happened anyway. My brother was born with a homing device for drugs. Self-medicating is only one symptom of his bipolar disorder. There's an old joke in AA: *The difference between an alcoholic and a drug addict is that an alcoholic will steal your wallet, while the drug addict will steal your wallet and help you look for it later.* In this way, the lies become the truth. They *are* his truth, the facts having crumbled to ash.

In Florida, it is morning and the three of us are weary. We must walk. We walk and hold hands on the beach. We look like the album cover for a family folk band. We meet a guy named Jeff. He lives "where the wind blows him, man." Says, "Woah, what's wrong with you, man?" I tell him I am sick. Jeff has a ponytail and bums a cigarette. We watch the ocean and smoke. We don't talk. Eric puts a towel over my shoulders. I think of the footage of a tsunami I watched recently. It was difficult not to sense some malevolent deity here, rising up and mouth agape, ready to swallow us for our sins.

Here we'd sit, waiting.

It is overcast today and the ocean wind blows back at us a warning. Palm trees shudder, a hint of sex, a flash of Mother Nature's fleshy thigh. In this light, I see now that Eric is going bald, fallibility rising to the surface. He digs his heels into the sand until his toes find water. *I can see it, Little Brother; almost there—China.* I watch desire working on his jaw, appetite gnawing every joint. He cannot sit still. *Here,* I want to scream, *is my surgeon's blade. Hold still and I'll cut the sickness out of every bone and suck them clean. Yours, mine. Here it is; here, I have it.*

Run.

Finally, Jeff gets up and says he has to get back to work. He washes dishes at a nearby restaurant. "My son needs a job," my mother blurts out. "Could you find him a job?" She is pleading, though I know it had not been her intention. Eric looks away, embarrassed.

"Sorry, man," Jeff says, and we can see that he is. "I'm lucky I got myself a job." He picks up his duffel bag and slings it over a broad, tanned shoulder. He looks over at me, slumping under the towel, staring and vacant. A job. Don't I have one of those somewhere? My own little plot to tend? His expression changes as he realizes what's really going on here, that this isn't just some half-baked family reunion, some pleasure cruise through the tropics, the three of us squatting on this beach, sans bathing suits and suntan lotion, *mid-August in Florida, for God's sake*, shivering in our sweat, bug-eyed from exhaustion.

This is not where we ought to be, beating our brains against the rocks on this shore and then standing back to survey the wreckage, wondering dumbly where we went wrong. *We are not helping him, are we?* Free dinners and a new pair of jeans won't do the trick. There is no reviving this horse, no A for effort, no stopping the ocean—be it so inclined—from reaching out right now and breaking our scrawny necks in two.

"You should get that fever checked out," Jeff says to me, turning to walk back up the beach. And then I, too, almost beg him to stay.

Later, we walk back to the motel, Eric leading us through the pearlescent, shrink-wrapped streets of Delray Beach, past the spit-shined bistros and fusion taquerias, feathery sago palms wrapped in hot white lights and poised, sentry-like, on every patio. Waiters stand in air-conditioned entranceways, pressed and tucked, surveying orders and women's formidable pumps. These women, I notice, totter, too.

And then on into the pink slums, where everything is shredded, jacked, and naked, and we feel free to come undone.

Another year passes—August to August—a year of rehabs, relapses, and incarcerations. A year of purgatory, a year of waiting for the death that never quite comes, but comes close so many times I nearly go mad. Our mother wears her grief like a slit gown. August 26, 2011. One last visit before I move to Vermont. She and I walk side by side on the New Jersey coastline, listening to the alarms howling in the distance, demanding our immediate departure in the days before what is supposed to be a devastating hurricane. Irene, they call her, and we hum her tune. *Come on, Irene.* We want to stay on, but evacuation orders eventually drive us from the tiny barrier island and back to our own homes, hundreds of miles apart. We have been living so long under the threat of disaster that its physical manifestation would be a relief, I think. We might welcome the winds and stand open-armed and knock-kneed while she weeps at our feet and shoves glass down our throats. Why the cutters cut and the jumpers jump and the junkies drive needles through their hearts, and why, one night in early August, I drink every drop of alcohol I can find in my cupboards and then vomit violently—that we might find a pain we can name and point to and say, *This* is it.

Irene comes and goes.

We wake. My mother, my brother, and me. We wake and wake and wake. *Give it to God*, they say, *that the curtains might close.*

NOTES
ON THE
NEVER
ENDING

My mother picks Eric up from the halfway house in Northeast Philly where he's been staying. It is 10 AM. The halfway house is the right side of a narrow duplex. Houses brick and broken. Next to the halfway house is the crack house. Next to the crack house is the whorehouse. Next to the whorehouse is a family with two adorable little girls. There is a picnic table beside the halfway house with a single clematis vine wrapped around its base. The second- and third-floor windows have bars. It is not a boisterous block. People don't gather on stoops or around the open doors of parked cars. Music isn't coming from windows or boom boxes; women aren't shouting. With the exception of the men from the halfway house, who sit on top of the picnic table and smoke, the few people on the street move quickly and deliberately.

You go about your business and you get gone.

As my mother idles out front, men wander in and out of the screen door, letting it slam against the doorframe every time. She watches for her son's face somewhere in this procession of baggy clothes and hunched shoulders. These are men from everywhere, of all ages. Men with dirty fingernails, mostly, and scraggly facial hair, and receding hairlines. Men with a sense of humor. Men without jobs. Men who make each other spaghetti at night. Men who watch movies in groups of ten, sitting on a sofa, stretched out on the floor. Fat men and very skinny men. Levi's and baseball caps. Transient men without lovers. Or men with ex-wives and children far away. They are as familiar to her as her ex-husband, and now, as her own child. She grew up with these men and these men stuck around. She thinks she knows these men well, how they think and why they do what they do.

It is tempting to put all of these men into a box and watch them not even try to get out. It is tempting to impose your expectations on them and watch them not care. It is tempting not to look at your own failures, which are often so fucking ordinary.

Eric plans to stay for a few days. Though he claims to be sober, he is not well. He is having trouble sleeping. He is depressed and lonely. He'd called our mother in hysterics last night and she agreed to pick him up, though she's nervous about it. He tends to unravel when he is with her. There is always the possibility of a scene or a relapse or that he will steal something of hers and use the money for drugs. Still, why should she not pick up her child in his time of need?

Wouldn't she do the same for Jess? he'd argued.

She would.

And wouldn't she do whatever it took to help her child? Her child?

Yes.

And without evidence he's been using, has she any right to accuse him?

She does not.

She takes Eric to the psychiatrist so that he might get some medication to help with his unbearable anxiety and depression, to a doctor who has treated our whole family at one time or another, a man well into his eighties and unprepared to deal with the history of an addict and a convict. It is one o'clock in the afternoon. He knew our father. He knows our grandfather. He's met us both before.

The doctor is wearing two different shoes today, Eric tells her later in the car—one black, one brown.

■

These details, all of these details—this is what I do not want to know anymore. Every story about Eric has an arc that threatens to catapult me into oblivion. I have to get off the ride. I watch the way these years have laid into my mother's body like an abusive lover; the ecstatic highs of his wellness and the crashing lows of his relapses. Who can stand this shit? Who would lie down only to be bullwhipped across the heart? Do it enough and you're apt to forget how else to be. That's you, the woman on the floor. There, still red from prayer.

I miss my brother. I love my brother, but I can't be near him. I pack my bags and keep my eyes on the ground, only glancing back.

■

After my mother brings Eric home from the psychiatrist's office, they have dinner and watch a movie. Eric sprawls on the sofa and gently pets the dog, who lies heavy on his feet. I call around 11 PM. "Oh, and how are you?" she asks, careful not to suggest the real reason for my call, as if I am in the habit of calling so late *just to chat.*

I need to know that everything is *okay*, that he's there, alive, and not breaking shit. I relapse sometimes, too.

Nick sits beside me on our bed and kisses my throat anxiously, needful. I should hang up the phone. I should turn to him. I should take off my pants and give myself over, but I can't, not yet.

■

She hands the phone to Eric. He tells me that I am in trouble, that he's spoken to our paternal grandfather, Harry, and he's very angry that I never call him. I can tell that Eric is delighting in my misbehavior, relieved that for once it isn't him in the hot seat.

"He's our grandfather, Jess. For God's sake, the man has cancer and he's lonely. He's sitting at home right now reading a book about Poland. We can at least call him once a month."

He's right, of course, and all of my reasons for not calling disintegrate beside these simple facts. He sounds like the adult, and I enjoy arguing with him and losing. He is being mature and I am not. I even take a little pleasure in his reprimands. It feels good to hear him be the voice of reason, even if I don't like what he is saying.

When I call him for our grandfather's number the next morning, Eric's phone is off.

I'm not sure what makes my mother suggest to Eric that he ask for Ativan, a benzodiazepine used to treat anxiety. I suppose it is the desperation in his face, his trembling hands as he lights one cigarette after another. Whatever her reasons, Eric returns from the doctor's office with a prescription for Ativan.

My mother sleeps soundly that night for the first time in weeks. Eric starts to feel better.

"My heart has finally stopped pounding," he tells her shortly before bed.

It is a warm night for early spring. She coughs her smoker's cough; the fan blows over her through the night. At dawn, she kicks at her blankets, coughs, and turns over. The dogs doze beside her bed. Around eight, she hears Eric coming up the stairs and smells smoke from his cigarette. He is mumbling to himself and she bolts upright.

October 11, 2011.

Nick and I are searching on the Internet for a place to rent in Vermont. He's been offered a job at the University of Vermont. He is not fond of Connecticut anymore, and not persuaded by the quick access to New York City on the Metro-North. I don't blame him, but I can't find work in Vermont, even while I love the idea. I'm reluctant to give up my modest-paying but secure teaching job at a nearby college. I can't commit to moving again. I can't decide. We search through the photos of mountainside bungalows and converted barns. Everything broken charms me. I like the vaulted ceilings with cracked beams, the wide wooden siding gone soft with age. Nick scoffs at the way I romanticize the dilapidated and scans through the fine print for utilities and maintenance costs. I will forgive a lack of indoor plumbing if the view is right. He won't go near a place with oil heat. Since I haven't said for certain if I'm moving, he has the say-so and I'm pouting. We take a break and walk around the corner for sandwiches. We're not talking much these days and it is wonderful. Instead, we listen to the ocean slam against the piles of empty oyster shells collecting by the docks, and the sizzle as it recedes. Metal casings clink against the masts of docked sailboats like wind chimes. These are my father's sounds, and for a moment I wonder what he'd counsel.

■

"Eric? What's going on?" she says.

"I can't," Eric says to Mom softly, "I can't find the cherry on my cigarette."

She gets up and opens the door. He stands there stooped, a lit cigarette dangling from his fingers, and she sees that everything has gone awry, suddenly and again.

She sits him on the sofa and says, "I'm making eggs."

His bottle of Ativan is almost empty. He must have taken over twelve. Plus a handful of Unisom, he admits. While she tries to find a pan, she listens to Eric ramble in the living room.

"I said Lexapro. I said my mother and sister both take Lexapro and Ativan. Must be the family cure," he says, "must be the family cure."

For whatever reason, this is the loop that sticks and he says it over and over, staring into a glass of water, curls of dog hair floating on top. *Must be the family cure, must be the family cure.*

■

I run errands all morning, preparing for our move to Vermont. "Forget work," Nick had said finally, late one night and after hours of conversation, the most we'd spoken in weeks. "You'll sit in that cabin and finish your fucking book. As long as it takes. We'll work it out." I knew he was right. The cabin we've rented is on the lake and so small we won't be able to entertain.

This is fine with Nick. The view obliterates rational thought, which I consider good for the soul. Vermont is an eight-hour drive or a two-hour flight from Philadelphia. I can be in my cabin in Vermont and make it to a Philadelphia hospital in four hours, give or take. I consider this line of thinking bad for the soul, and look forward to morning coffee in front of the lakeside window. When I talk to my mother now she is enmeshed in Eric's daily dramas—his breakups and job losses and missing IDs and parole violations and backaches and lies and bowel movements and money woes and yet another girl's possibly positive pregnancy test. She pays his rent at the halfway house when she knows she should not. She buys his cigarettes and fills his cupboards with nonperishable food items. She takes him to his court hearings and to the methadone clinic. She calls me and says she has to have a cancer removed from her lip. She calls and says she has bronchitis. She calls and says she has a fractured knee. She calls and says she has shingles. She calls and I cringe.

■

Mom dumps the half-fried eggs in the trash and walks upstairs to call an ambulance. Eric protests weakly from the sofa. She does not panic. She does not yell. She moves slowly and purposefully. Seconds after she hangs up the phone the sirens begin to trill in the distance. She comes back downstairs. Eric looks up at her.

"I guess I should put on my shoes," he says.

■

Maybe I worry about stasis because it fails to distract me from whatever is looming in my family's future. Nick is nothing if not static, content, solid. I would like to sit still for a while. By a window. In Vermont. It's tough. Eric's relapses ring like a keening bell and I either sit still and listen or get loud.

Flap, flap, flap, I say to Nick. *Do something!* I cry. *Move!*

Every time the phone rings, I panic. Every time the phone rings, Eric is dead.

■

The sirens grow louder and closer. A spring day hurtles on. But here, right now, the kitchen smells of fried eggs and Windex and the refrigerator hums. The wooden floors are sun-warmed and Eric blinks, his eyes like jelly, black and pink. I am asleep, three hundred and eighty-four miles north and splayed naked, Nick's breath on my neck and my cell phone under my pillow. It won't ring, mercifully, for another three hours.

An ambulance arrives. The police come with the ambulance, standard protocol. A warrant is located; who knows what this one is for? A cop apologizes to my mother. They'll have to take him in. Handcuffs are drawn slowly from a cop's thick black belt. Eric hunches over on the front stoop. The dogs clamber over themselves to get to his lap, to lick his chin. Back to jail. Back to jail. Back, back, back.

"Fuck," she says. "Fuck." The cop is gentle. He puts a hand on her shoulder. "He's sick," she says. "Please don't take him. He's sick."

"Your son is very polite," the cop says. "They're not usually so polite."

"Please don't be mad," Eric whispers into our mother's ear. She hugs him.

"Please don't count this as a relapse," he begs. "I had eight months."

Like hell, she thinks.

"Yes," she says.

"I'll see you soon," he says. "This isn't a relapse."

"Yes," she says. "Okay."

And for the first time, she lets him go.

That night, Nick and I take a walk. He holds my hand. We watch people stumble in and out of bars. We watch the lights change: red, yellow, green. We are tired, but content. We ate well. Eric is in jail, but alive.

In the morning, Nick will load his U-Haul with six boxes and an air mattress and drive to our cabin in Vermont. He'll start his new job as a health care researcher and I will finish up the semester at the State University of New York, where I've been teaching for the past year and a half. I'll join him on New Year's Day, driving out of our old neighborhood through the sea of confetti lapping at the streets. On the highway, the landscape changes slowly, then all at once. My little truck strains to climb the steep inclines, then barrels down and down with abandon. Mountains charge into the clouds on either side of the empty road. Driving alone, I feel cradled inside something both tender and cruel. I watch the temperature gauge on the truck's dashboard tick down the degrees, one every ten minutes or so. I turn off the radio. I smooth my hair and adjust my gaping sweater, as if it matters. My foot flattens the gas pedal as I try to push the truck up another mountainside, beside a crevasse draped in daggers of ice.

THE
END
OF THE
EARTH

MID-FEBRUARY, 2012, AND Mallets Bay is frozen over, the small enclave of Lake Champlain that stretches out in front of our cabin in Vermont like a slow yawn. I spend the better part of an hour listening to the mice tittering in the walls. When Nick gets home from work he opens up an electrical socket, places a hunk of cheese into a trash bag, and tapes the bag around the hole. He doesn't care—he hates cheese—but my heart breaks a little. For three hours, we entertain ourselves by listening to the mice scurry in and out of the bag, absconding with my good Piave. I squeal every time I hear the rustling, until finally Nick closes off the bag and scoops its contents into a drinking glass. The mouse blinks rapidly and then settles back to gaze at us with bored resignation.

"He's terrified," Nick says.

"I'm terrified," I say.

"This was a bad idea," he says, and heads outside with the mouse.

I follow him down the street and watch as he gently pours the mouse into the snow. It twitches once and takes off toward the lake, stops, thinks better of it, and skitters back up to our cabin.

"That's your problem," I say. "You show too much mercy."

It is so quiet that tonight, from our living room, we can hear the ice groan as it splits and shifts and freezes again. It sounds like thunder, or a whale song, some distant cry of the belugas that lived in the lake ten thousand years ago. There are fossils to prove it. We open all the windows and sit by the woodstove with our eyes closed, listening. Later, he leads me down to the lake and we shuffle onto the ice and watch the stars. I keep hearing the ice crack, jagged pings from here to the mouth of the bay. I am sure it will give out at any moment and we'll be sucked under, left to hold eternal court with the slow bass bellying along in their winter stupor. I keep picturing our faces bobbing lightly against the underside of an ice floe while, in some nearby shanty, a grizzled angler slurps his morning coffee and tunes the channels on his portable television. Nick laughs and says, "It's fine, it's fine," and "Why so dramatic?"

Pardon me, but I am my mother's daughter after all.

This is his country, my mountain man, and he is all ease. I keep forgetting not to ask about the tide schedule. I'm not yet convinced that there aren't any sharks.

I SHIVER IN my dreams and wake to the sound of the phone ringing at 4 AM. It is my friend in Queens. We used to be roommates. She stayed in New York and made a life there, while I took off after graduating from Sarah Lawrence College, MFA in tow. I was too lonely in the city, too overwhelmed. Like an overstimulated child, I couldn't block things out, narrow the focus. Edit. Instead, I took it all in, all the time. A friend once told me that New Yorkers have mastered the art of being publicly private. New York made me crazy and tired. In rare moments of quiet I became paranoid, a strange specter in empty subway terminals searching for rats scurrying across the tracks. I made a game of it. If I couldn't spot one before the train arrived, I'd be doomed to mediocrity forever, or something equally torturous. I still visit my friend often, though, and she keeps the guest room ready for me, my earplugs on the nightstand, my name scribbled on the box in black Sharpie. We eat large meals in small restaurants and pay for them with our credit cards. Before bed, she hands me a glass of water and kisses me on the mouth. She would be a wonderful mother, but at thirty-seven, she relishes her independence, the ability to pick up and go when the mood strikes, lavishing all those maternal instincts on wayward friends like me.

Now she is upset, she says, and needs to talk. The police showed up at her apartment a couple hours ago, around two. She had been awake and reading and noticed lights flashing on her bedroom walls. Her small dog yipped and snarled, running frantically from window to bed and back again, his whole body shaking. It is not so cold in New York this winter, and she had her windows cracked open because the landlords, who live below her in the brownstone, like to keep the heat up high. I've met them a few times—an attractive couple in their early forties with a two-year-old daughter, a small girl with tight curls of red hair and three pill-sized teeth. They fight often and loudly. The husband has beautiful tattoos covering both arms and his wife is a psychiatrist who once kindly offered me Lexapro samples when I'd forgotten to pack my own.

My friend watched flashlights move from the front of the house to the back. She heard the low muffling of voices and the beeping of walkie-talkies. Her roommate, a waiter who works late nights at a posh Manhattan restaurant with a temperamental celebrity chef, was still at work.

She heard clomping up the stairs and grabbed the dog just as one of the cops flung open her front door, left unlocked for the roommate who never remembers his key. The high beams of the flashlights bounced around her backyard.

"You seen some cops around here?" he asked.

"They're in the backyard," she said. "What's going on?"

Without answering, the young cop turned and bounded back downstairs. She thought there may have been a break-in and she locked her door behind him, an afterthought. She considered the confrontation the husband had had with a neighbor just a few days before, something about a parking spot. It could have been anything, she said.

"What's going on?" she yelled again, this time through the door, but the cop continued to ignore her. She walked to the back window and drew open the curtains. She could see Manhattan lit up in the distance like a carnival. She's grown to love this skyline and the adventures it dangles in front of her, even while she spends most of her free time holed up inside the apartment, reading books and watching movies while the dog dozes on her belly. She is a California girl, *a country bumpkin at heart*, she insists, but her hippie parents also instilled gypsy tendencies that render her helpless to the lure of the new and better. Like me, she jumps state lines every few years.

She'd pulled her red hair into a knot in order to see more clearly. A small purple bicycle leaned against the fence and an abandoned bottle of bubbles lay sideways on the picnic table. Some leftover streamers from a recent birthday party hung limp from a tree branch. Below her, she saw the flat white blade of a stretcher illuminated on the patio, and then draping over the side of a deck chair was a single arm, tattooed in faded reds and blues.

Here she pauses and breathes deeply into the phone line. I realize I am still in bed next to Nick, who is sleeping with one leg drawn up to his chest like an unspent arrow. I get up, wrap myself in a quilt, and open the front door. I hear the bed creak as Nick rolls over in his sleep. I sit down on the front steps. A neighbor is getting into his mail truck, readying himself for the day. He has a cup of coffee and a cigarette. I am still half-asleep, a dull anxiety thrumming its way up my throat. The postman sits in his truck while the engine idles and warms, the exhaust from his tailpipe fogging up the windows of his cabin. A slice of dawn catches the mast of a sailboat moored for winter beside the docks.

My neighbor nods hello and backs out of his driveway, turning left at the lake.

LATER THAT MORNING, the cold wakes me up again, as it has almost every day since I arrived here from the tumbling beach town in Connecticut where I'd been pleasantly discontented. I'd had a job, at least, which is more than I have now. This is our seventh home in the eight years we've been together, and for the first time, it's on his terms. He likes New England best, despite my argument that he ought to see more of the country before he makes that decision. I'm inclined to agree, though; I like New England best, too. I'm just not ready for the picket fence. I'm into fucking around, slowly dragging us further south since we left New Hampshire after college. But suddenly, in one fell swoop, we're all the way up in northern Vermont—an hour from *Canada*, for christsake—and I'm cold and bitter and cold. I resolve to act like a brat for another couple of weeks and then I'll have to let it go.

Truth is, I'm living off the fat of the land, as they say, though it is an odd metaphor in a landscape so doggedly hard. Spring will arrive eventually, the land will soften, the garden will murmur and open, but not yet. I prefer to call myself a kept woman, joking with my friends, which at least bears the whiff of silk robes and a leased Lamborghini. In reality, I roll out of bed hours after Nick has left for work. I sit huddled next to the stove and write for as long as I can stand it. I take long walks in the middle of the day, and in the afternoon, cook elaborate dinners that taste like shit. The cooking is a way to avoid the writing, which is all I want to do and the one thing I don't want to do. The cabin we've rented is charming and falling to pieces. The woman who owns it has a famous daughter and a summer place fifty yards away. Few people in this neighborhood are foolish enough to stay on all winter and those that do keep hay bales stacked against the siding as insulation. I like watching the way they live through my window, drowning in coffee, crying when I damn well feel like it—benefits of this solitary lifestyle. We keep the woodstove running all day and use a space heater at night, avoiding the expense of oil heat. I'd throw a fit except I'm not paying any bills, so instead I shiver wildly and refuse to take off my wool cap. I'd surprised myself by following him here and I'm not ready to admit that I'm staying. When he got the job as a researcher at a nearby university, he decided he would take it, with or without me, and I'm still adjusting to his new confidence.

It's Saturday morning so the frozen bay looks like a theme park. Kids in oversized coats skate in clusters and fall on top of each other and laugh and whine and shout. A group of teenagers play hockey beside the docks, between the old Christmas trees that stick out of the ice like broken toothpicks. No one knows how they got there, or at least they're not saying. Wooden shanties lean precariously while fishermen gather in tight circles around a single drilled hole, chatting and smoking and swigging from cans of beer.

When we first slide onto the ice, I shimmy like a toddler before I realize that it isn't so slippery after all. It feels strange and illicit to stand in the middle of the lake and look up at the mountains towering in the distance. Mount Mansfield winks at us from behind a veil of clouds. In the summer, I will climb her ridges like a tethered donkey, and later this winter, ride her broadside on a pair of rented skis. That's the thing I'm learning about savage landscapes: intimacy is inevitable.

Vermonters interact with the land in more ways than I've witnessed in other places. Winter sports are not just recreation; they keep you sane. And while Vermonters are a notoriously self-reliant people, the weather is a shared and worthy adversary. They work together to beat back the snowdrifts, to till the hard soil, to bring produce to market. Once, when my car was stuck trying to ascend a hill during a snowstorm, an entire block of neighbors shoveled sand under my tires while I gunned the engine and teenagers pushed the car from behind. After half an hour, and more than one lecture on snow tires, we were regular good-time buddies.

An iceboat whips by, carving two thin parallel lines. A gust of wind catches her sails and the whole job topples over, splayed out like a crippled bird. I feel suddenly excited, electric, turned on. The sun is high and I'm feeling safer on the ice. Here are the natives, running wild and fearless. Still, I move gingerly and watch Nick glide in his sneakers like an overgrown kid. I'm still shaken by the late-night phone call; images from my friend's story are reverberating through my head, projecting on the ice like a silent film.

Where the ice has frozen and refrozen it is white and opaque, pentagon-shaped pancakes, and in other places it is like a clear glass, struck through with the bent bodies of dead pickerel, old fishing lures, and leftover autumn leaves still a brilliant burnt orange. Nick's hat falls from his head and as he reaches to pick it up, he loses his balance and falls to the ice. His camera goes skidding and he rolls over, legs and arms splayed, defeated and grinning at the sky. Silver in his dark hair and red in his beard and eyes a burnished blue. A thin-lipped, long-lashed beauty. Contemplative and quiet. I want to make love to him right there on the ice. Thankfully, he has more discretion.

There is a stress fracture in the ice about a half mile from where we stand. I know it is a stress fracture because Nick told me. I had thought it was something else: the end of the earth.

"From the tide change?" I offer, but he only shakes his head.

Nick says that the only time I want to have sex is when we're in public. We spend the next fifteen minutes theorizing on why this is, Nick suggesting it's just some misplaced voyeurism, while I insist it's probably more perverse than that. We make our way toward the stress fracture, drawn by the reflection of the sun on the sharp chunks of ice that stick up in the air. Increasingly, it looks like a line of fire splitting the lake in two. Beyond it, men are playing hockey with one net. Someone rolls a keg onto the lake and a camera flashes and one of the men yells out, "Crack her open, Gibbons made a shot!" For a moment, I wish Nick were the type of man to play hockey with friends and drink beers and chuckle deeply, elbowing buddies in the ribs. I like to watch men with other men, all those precious manners trimmed away like excess fat. Instead, he is all sweetness and gentility, a time traveler having lost his way.

As we get closer, I see the men have finished their game and are standing around reciting blow-by-blows. It is late afternoon and the sun is melting the top layer of ice, though there are still a good twelve inches below us. Surely, I think, I have chosen wisely this time—this small life and its reassuring rhythms and routines. It all feels so *wholesome*, the kids on their skates and the mothers eyeing them from shore, handing out granola bars and kisses when they fall. It was nothing I ever imagined for myself, but here I am.

"I could raise kids here," I tell Nick, feeling suddenly flush with gratitude.

It is undeserved, I am sure, but maybe I can do this— absolve myself of my brother's debilitating addictions, the calamitous city, my own desperate ambitions and depression. We'll grow our own vegetables and *volunteer in the community*. What a thought. I can hear my mother laughing, her brow cocked in suspicion. But the brutality of the weather and the inhospitableness of the land seem to bring people together here, a hardscrabble let-me-help-you-with-that type of thing, which I think might make me a better person, too. The kind who bakes casseroles for ailing neighbors and untangles your fishing line. I cannot fix my family, but I can learn to fix an edible dinner. I want to know the names of the people at the gym and at the bank. Their kids' names, too. Isn't Vermont the kind of place where people do that? Where the local handyman will pat your ailing woodstove and coo, "It's all right, girl, just having a bad hair day, is all."

Having grown up in a small New England town, Nick sees a different side to all this camaraderie, how nobody can keep their fingers out of anyone else's pie. He draws our curtains tight at night and shushes me quiet when I laugh too loud or call out from our bed. He doesn't understand the safety I feel here, and how little of it I've known. Does spring not return here, too, eventually? I insist. Does the lake ice not come apart, the leaves not unfurl from weather-beaten branches, predictably, annually? It had not been like this in the city—Philly or Manhattan—where the only signs of renewal seemed relegated to the margins, the dandelions poking up through cracks in the sidewalk, grasses muted in their designated six-by-four plots. Yes, I can make a go of it here. I can learn to mollify myself with routine—now the seven o'clock news, now the beef stew. Here, your Sunday paper.

"Don't get ahead of yourself," Nick warns me. "You've been here less than a month."

But I know this is what he wants, has always wanted, and my new openness is both heartening and scary for him. I, too, have the gypsy in me—a restlessness we have both grown to fear.

By the time my friend made it to the bottom of her steps, the landlady was in the hallway with the child clutched in her arms, a gaggle of police officers beside her. The child was in her pajamas and her winter coat and looked wide-awake, even though it was after two in the morning.

"I have to go to the hospital," the woman cried out to my friend. "He tried to kill himself."

My friend was relieved that her landlord was still alive, and frightened for the small girl, her arms wrapped tightly around her mother's neck, though she seemed calm. She looked up at my friend and reached for her, even though they had no more than a passing acquaintance. The woman was crying and my friend hugged her tightly, the girl pressed between them.

"Do you want me to take the baby?" my friend asked.

She didn't see the sense in dragging the child to the hospital in the middle of the night just to watch her daddy suffer, or possibly even die. She was surprised when the landlady said yes, thrusting the child into her arms before reeling through the front door, the cops following behind her obediently. She heard radios screeching and a succession of car doors slamming, and then the cry of the ambulance as it tore off into the night. Soon, it was all over. The child in her arms sat placidly sucking on a pacifier now, her fingers coiled into my friend's hair.

"Well," she said to her, "shall we go to bed, honey?"

The child laid her head on my friend's chest. For a moment, she didn't know where to take her. Her apartment? Theirs? What was in there? What had the child seen? While her landlord had been in the backyard, she didn't know what could have happened inside, if any of the night's detritus would be left out for the child, or her, to see. She slowly opened the door to their apartment. Better that she sleep in her own bed, she thought.

"My sweet girl," my friend whispered. "You poor sweet girl."

I try for calm while the ice moans beneath us. I hold Nick's hand and try to feel comfort in the simple gesture, the security in our time together, past and future. My legs tense as we slide on top of the lake. We are miniature dolls in the shadow of the mountains, time before time. The bottoms of my feet are so cold they feel disconnected from the rest of my body. The wind races through the valley, shooting sprays of snow from the piles on shore. Pure energy dissolving into dust.

Though I don't know it yet, back home in Philadelphia my family is coming apart again. My brother lies in a hospital bed with our mother beside him. He's had his first overdose. He'd left rehab with a girl, their twinned hearts racing as they drove straight into the underbelly of the city. This morning, as I sat outside on the cabin steps and listened to my friend cry quietly into the phone, afraid to wake the child who had finally fallen asleep; while I watched the sun patiently rise behind the lake, and the mailman set about his rounds, and a mottled robin peck at the seeds fallen from the birdfeeder onto the frozen ground, my brother's breathing shallowed like a receding wave. His heart seized and his skin drew blue and the tiny scalloped muscles behind his eyes began to quiver. When the girl found him in her living room, a boy she barely knew, a wretched shucked thing, turned out and writhing in his own puke, I'd crept back into our warm bed and returned to sleep, unaware.

I am delighting in the weight of the slabs of ice that formed in the seam of the lake. They are both homage to and mockery of the great mountains that surfaced from glacial shifts so long ago. I pick them up and hurl them back down to shatter into a million shots of light, while Nick captures the destruction, and my ecstatic reaction to this destruction, with his camera, the shutter clicking and clicking while the sounds of the people hush and go flat. There is only the breaking—heave and crack, heave and crack—so loud that neither of us hears the lake open up beneath me, sees my boot slip two inches too close and the water rise up past my ankles, my calves, the thick fabric of my ski pants swelling and drawing me under, heavy as an anchor. We don't realize what is happening until it has happened, until the panic is in my throat and the camera slips out of Nick's hands and I feel (not *feel* exactly, but *sense*) the icy water filling my clothes, gripping my thighs; and there is no thought but dreams, the way that dreams will take the shape of recent, but not too recent, memories. A child sitting completely still on her parents' bed, her red hair lit up by the streetlight coming in through the window, staring into the backyard where her father acted out his private despair, my friend frozen in the doorway, the child too young to communicate what she knows or how she knows it, what it feels like inside a dread so private it can only be expressed this way—the body fighting instinctively for what the mind has all but given up. My father, her father, fathers falling. Sometimes, there is a note glowing on a computer screen in a dark room. More often, the message is beyond language, or pre-language.

A girl holds a boy's hand in an ambulance.

A wife, her husband's.

A mother, her son's.

A childless woman wraps her body around a small girl on an unfamiliar bed in a city where such intimacies seem suddenly inevitable. Only *here*, my friend thinks. Only in this place, this city, with all these hot souls drawn together to thrive or suffer or go under—but we'll be damned if we'll go unwitnessed.

I make love loudly, I told Nick once, because you want to hear it and I need to say it. We suffer, but I am happy right now, and I am safe in this moment. I needn't feel guilty about that. I've run away before. Believe me, I will do it again.

Believe me, I will not want to.

I sit in the shower and let the hot water thaw my skin. Nick had dragged me out of the icy water and worn my wet boots to shore. My feet felt small and numb inside his dry boots. A bruise forms on my thigh where I fell. It will remain there for weeks, a caution: *Don't get ahead of yourself.* My hero makes soup in the kitchen. The child is returned to her mother, bathed and fed and resolutely silent. My friend climbs the stairs to her apartment and falls into bed while water puddles between my toes and my brother is pumped through with Propofol. Her roommate tries the locked door and realizes he has forgotten his key.

He knocks, but she is already asleep.

My mother holds her son's hand while he breathes through a tube, sedated. She reaches into her purse for a cigarette and her phone, and then heads toward the door. I hear the soup bubbling in the pan and I watch a spider cling to her web in the corner of the shower. In another moment, my phone will ring. Nick will bring it into the bathroom and hold it out to me.

"Your mother," he will say. "You want it?"

I watch her picture grinning on the screen, radiant in last summer's sun. I hear the mice in the wall.

"I'll call her back," I say. He nods and kisses my forehead.

"Dinnertime," he says. "When you're ready."

ACKNOWLEDGMENTS

I am forever in gratitude to my family and friends who have shared their stories in the pages of this book.

For the love and support, always: Susan Nelson, Eric Nelson, Helen Gordon (I love you, Mommom!), Carole Gordon, Adam Gordon, Denise Gordon-Weisman, Jessie McLaughlin (M&N), Hannah Campbell, Angela Palm, Greg Falla, Aryn Hood, Meredith Grinnell, Ellen and Lou Vitola, Debra Hoffman, Nick Adams and the whole Adams family.

Thank you to Andrew Merton and Meredith Hall, who provided the tools and encouragement that have sustained me these many years. To my mentors and guides, Jo Ann Beard, Vijay Seshadri, and Alice Truax. To my steadfast agent, Joanne Wyckoff, editor extraordinaire, Dan Smetanka, and the incredible team at Counterpoint Press. What a gift. To everyone in the Renegade Writers' Group who helped shape these pages.

In loving memory of Irving Gordon, Cynthia Ann Turner, Harry Nelson, and my father, Jonathan Robert Nelson.